P9-CFC-303

BOOKS BY IRVING HOWE

A Margin of Hope
Celebrations and Attacks
Leon Trotsky
World of Our Fathers
(with the assistance of Kenneth Libo)
The Critical Point
Decline of the New
Steady Work: Essays in the Politics of Democratic Radicalism, 1953–1966
Thomas Hardy: A Critical Study
A World More Attractive
The American Communist Party: A Critical History
(with Lewis Coser)
Politics and the Novel
William Faulkner: A Critical Study
Sherwood Anderson: A Critical Biography
The U.A.W. and Walter Reuther
(with B. J. Widick)

BOOKS EDITED BY IRVING HOWE

How We Lived
(with Kenneth Libo)
The World of the Blue-Collar Worker
Essential Works of Socialism
The Seventies: Problems & Proposals
(with Michael Harrington)
Voices from the Yiddish
(with Eliezer Greenberg)
A Treasury of Yiddish Poetry
(with Eliezer Greenberg)
The Idea of the Modern
The Basic Writings of Trotsky
The Radical Imagination
Edith Wharton: A Critical Collection
The Radical Papers
A Treasury of Yiddish Stories
(with Eliezer Greenberg)

Irving Howe

SOCIALISM and AMERICA

A HARVEST/HBJ BOOK
HARCOURT BRACE JOVANOVICH, PUBLISHERS
SAN DIEGO NEW YORK LONDON

"Socialism and Liberalism: Articles of Conciliation?" and "Thinking about Socialism" first appeared in slightly different form in *Dissent.*

Library of Congress Cataloging in Publication Data
Howe, Irving.
Socialism and America.
Bibliography: p.
1. Socialism—United States. 2. Socialism—United States—History. I. Title.
HX86.H794 1985 335'.00973 85-8691
ISBN 0-15-183575-6
ISBN 0-15-683520-7 (Harvest/HBJ : pbk.)

Designed by G.B.D. Smith

Printed in the United States of America

First Harvest/HBJ edition 1986

A B C D E F G H I J

For Michael Harrington
and Michael Walzer

Contents

Preface

This book offers historical material about American socialism, but it is not a history of that movement. It offers, in its second part, essays intended as a modest contribution toward the renewal of socialist thought, but it is not a full-scale examination of socialist thought. What sort of book is it, then?

My deepest feeling about this book is that, in a certain sense, it has neither a beginning nor an end. It forms part of a continuing discussion, sometimes in the form of reassertion and sometimes in the form of self-criticism, that has been going on among democratic socialists for some decades and will surely continue for decades to come. All major world-views or political tendencies making any claim to intellectual seriousness are committed to a similar exercise. Sustained self-scrutiny, hard self-criticism, and, perhaps in consequence, a partial self-renewal: these are the order of the day.

An uninitiated reader coming to this book may see her(him)-self as someone overhearing a stream of dialogue or reflection.

Even for a reader who strongly disagrees, this can have a strong interest—provided, of course, the stream of dialogue or reflection seems worth listening to. And that, of course, each reader will judge for him(her)self. At the same time, I believe this book can be read apart from the tradition to which it is linked—can be read as a self-sufficient work of analysis and opinion.

What has impelled me to write has been a need to confront the question: Why did American socialism thrive at some moments and decline at others? To confront a question doesn't necessarily mean to come up with a quick or assured answer; sometimes it can mean quite the opposite. It can mean redefining a question or modifying previous answers, or even deciding there aren't any satisfactory answers. And to confront the question I have posed, as well as some tributary questions, I have provided what I think is enough historical material to make the discussion intelligible.

There is only one kind of unity that finally matters in a book—the unity of a problem steadily considered and engaged.

I.H.

Acknowledgments

The first three chapters of this book were originally given as the W. W. Cook lectures at the University of Michigan Law School in 1981. Appearing here for the first time in print, they have been extensively revised and enlarged. But I could not even have begun to undertake this project without the kind invitation for the Cook lectures extended by the dean of the Law School at Michigan, Terrance Sandalow.

In completing this book, I was able to take time off from my teaching obligations because of a grant provided by the Ford Foundation. And, again, I wish to offer my thanks.

My greatest debt is to Mark Levinson, a brilliant young economist who served as research assistant and watchful critic for this book. Portions of the manuscript have been read and helpfully criticized by friends: Joseph Clark, Lewis Coser, Emanuel Geltman, Michael Harrington, Robert Heilbroner, Robert Lekachman, and Michael Walzer. My thanks to them.

The two concluding chapters have appeared, in slightly different form, in *Dissent*. A few sentences in the first chapter have been borrowed from *The American Communist Party: A Critical History*, by Lewis Coser and me.

PART ONE

Socialism and America

The Era of Debs

Let us stop the clock at 1912, a pretty good year for American socialists. I stop there if only because we will soon have to move to other years that were not so good. With an all-time peak membership of about 118,000, the Socialist Party polled 879,000 votes in the 1912 election, or nearly 6 percent of the total. More than a thousand socialists had been elected to office: there was a congressman from Wisconsin, Victor Berger; there were mayors in Butte, Montana; Berkeley, California; Flint, Michigan; there were many members in state legislatures. Some of these elected officials came straight from the ranks of the American working class: the mayor of Flint was a cigarmaker; the mayor of New Castle, Pennsylvania, a railroad brakeman; the mayor of Saint Marys, Ohio, a machinist.

Over three hundred English- and foreign-language publications, some painfully crude but others quite sophisticated, spread the socialist message. There were five socialist dailies in English and eight in other languages; 262 weeklies in English, thirty-six in other languages; ten monthlies in English, two in other languages. The total circulation of this press has been estimated as more than two million: the weekly *Appeal to Reason,* published in Kansas, had an average circulation of over 750,000; the *National Ripsaw,* blending socialist and populist appeals to farmers, 150,000; the *Jewish Daily Forward,* nearly 150,000; the *Texas Rebel,* 26,000; the daily *Milwaukee Leader,* 35,000. In Oklahoma alone there were eleven socialist weeklies by 1913.

Eclectic, vivid, impassioned, erratic, this press offered schematic lessons in Marxist economics side by side with essays on popular science; fierce calls to direct revolutionary action with bland Christian moralizing. Some of these papers appealed to segments of the population just breaking into literacy, others to immigrants for whom the coming triumph of socialism seemed indistinguishable from their coming rise on the social ladder.

In the *Appeal to Reason* American socialism found its most indigenous voice. Hawked by a nation-wide "Appeal Army," this paper expressed both an unspoiled idealism and the naïveté of a poorly digested Marxism. Bubbling with ingenuous enthusiasm, it spoke in rich homespun accents. It was remarkable, also, for its air of certainty, its lack of reflectiveness.

A torrent of pamphlets poured out of the socialist national office in Chicago. Speakers, organizers, part-time volunteers toured and tramped across the country. Socialist lyceums sprang up as part of that urge to self-improvement which swept America during the early years of the century. The socialist hall, where bundles of "literature" lay stacked, became a familiar landmark in hundreds of cities and towns.

At the 1912 convention of the American Federation of Labor,

Max Hayes, a socialist printer from Cleveland, won a third of the vote for president against the powerful incumbent, Samuel Gompers, apostle of bread-and-butter unionism. The socialists controlled, or were strong in, such important unions as the Western Federation of Miners, the Brewery Workers, the Machinists, the Jewish garment unions. Openly declared socialists presided over the Illinois and Pennsylvania federations of labor. The AFL was still far from being socialist in its dominant outlook, but the socialists formed a significant minority within it.

Thousands of rank-and-filers performed the daily routine of the party with a religious devotion. At least as great an asset was the party's spokesman, Eugene Victor Debs, an orator able to establish a rapport with the American people such as no other radical in this country has ever had. Pouring out his call to brotherhood and revolt—the two for him inseparable—Debs made the slogans of radicalism vibrate with truth and beauty and hope: the very slogans that in the mouths of others could seem the merest rhetoric.

The American socialist movement was not yet a mass movement: it did not command the support of a major portion of the working class, as some European social democratic parties did. But it had taken a few large steps from the isolation of the left-wing sect. It breathed an aura of hope and expectation, sharing in the optimistic mood of the country as a whole, where Progressivism as sentiment and movement was at a high point and the culture was bubbling with rebellious impulse. As Debs fired vast meetings, thousands of Americans were convinced that the growth of "the party" would continue in a benevolent progression toward the cooperative commonwealth. Behind every word of the socialists, as of most other Americans, lay the unspoken assumption of Progress. Yet, within six or seven years, the Socialist Party would be in shambles, with many of its leaders imprisoned, its organization torn apart by government repression, its ranks split into warring factions, and thousands of the faithful bewildered and demoralized. What, it seems worth asking, could happen to undo so promising a movement? Before going ahead to the years of World War I, we must turn back a little for a critical anatomy of Debsian socialism.

When one considers the inner diversity—indeed, the chaos of conflicting opinions, styles, accents, and levels of thought—within the Debsian Socialist Party, the most remarkable thing about it is that it ever held together. How could they all stay in the same party—the stolid social democrats of Wisconsin with the fierce syndicalists of the West, the Jewish immigrant workers of New York with the inflamed tenant farmers of Oklahoma, the Christian socialists with the orthodox Marxists?

One answer is so simple that most historians have tended to neglect it. In the years before World War I the regional distinctions that figure so strongly in our culture were still real, not a mere indulgence of nostalgia. Distance mattered. What a socialist local did in the coal-mining town of Krebs, Oklahoma, seldom touched a Yiddish-speaking branch on the Lower East Side of New York. What moderate comrades did to win elections in Reading, Pennsylvania, seldom had much importance for the tough left-wingers in the Western Federation of Miners. Victor Berger, the "revisionist" leader of the German-immigrant social democracy in Milwaukee, somehow coexisted—at least until 1912—with Big Bill Haywood, the Wobbly hero preaching "direct action," which, he did not mince words, often meant violence. The country was large; it took a few days to get from New York to Oklahoma.

The sentiment of regionalism was as strong in the Socialist Party as it was in the United States generally. Eventually, when overriding national issues had to be confronted, this would prove to be a source of grave troubles for the party. At the moment, the regionalism that kept comrades somewhat apart also enabled them to stay somewhat together.

The national office of the party was mostly a clearinghouse for propaganda. It's even a question whether one could really speak of a coherent national leadership. Debs was loved by many and criticized by some, but he chose to keep aloof from organizational life and party disputes; he made it a practice to stay away from party conventions—by democratic standards, a dubious practice. This enabled him to avoid problems he wasn't always intellectually equipped to confront, and it was also, to some extent, good for the party since it gave Debs a position from which to serve as unifying figure above factions, the spokesman who embodied its larger ideals. One might almost say that the Debsian party was really a confederation of regional baronies that sometimes coincided with, but also crisscrossed, ideological tendencies. Week by week, these regional baronies pretty much went their own ways.

The firmest of the baronies was located in Wisconsin, drawing upon descendents of exiles from autocratic Germany. A good many of the Milwaukee comrades were skilled AFL craftsmen for whom social democracy was both a cause and a culture. Sober, well organized, attentive to municipal detail, these "sewer socialists," as leftist critics sneeringly called them, had little of the millennial zeal that marked the Debsian cadres in the West and Southwest. They had achieved something, however, that no other segment of the movement quite did: they lived in close harmony with, and enjoyed the support of, the local trade unions, thereby overcoming that disastrous hostility between party and union which has been the curse of American socialism. Victor Berger, the leader of the Wisconsin socialists, was a disagreeable man, vain, boastful, acerbic, but also a shrewd political tactician. The somewhat pedestrian social democrats of Wisconsin, even with their German accents, had intuitively grasped the sentiments of those many Americans who desired an accumulation of reforms but were put off by the rhetoric of revolution. They seldom rose to the rebellious lyricism of Debs; but in the end they showed a keener apprehension of the developing changes in American society than such fundamentalist and utterly indigenous radicals as the "Texas reds," the Oklahoma rebels, the Colorado syndicalists.

Sharply different from the Wisconsin socialists in tone and temperament, though fairly close in formal opinion, was the cluster of Jewish immigrant socialists in New York. By about 1910 the Jewish socialists—a strong minority and probably the most vital political segment within the immigrant Jewish community—were starting to learn the arts of electoral politics. A few decades earlier they had begun with the sterile accents of a "universalistic" radicalism, denying—in Yiddish, of course—that their socialism had a distinctively Jewish character; but in a few years they had moved closer to the position of the Bundists, or Jewish socialists from Russian Poland, who had come to New York as refugees from the 1905 Russian Revolution and were trying to link socialist politics with Yiddish culture. The result had been a quickening of militancy and a growth of sophistication within the Jewish socialist ranks. Intense and excitable, with a loftiness of spirit even its opponents envied, New York socialism gave the Jewish garment workers a sense of home and of mission. The leader of Jewish socialism was Morris Hillquit, a complex and reflective man, who regarded himself as a Marxist in the tradition of Karl Kautsky and the German social democracy, and who kept soberly trying to steer the erratic American movement between the extremes of antipolitical syndicalism and incoherent reform.

The Jewish socialists kept picking up strength, but mostly within the immigrant milieu; never did they manage to gain more than a few pockets of Irish, German, and native-American support. The very successes they scored on the Lower East Side made them realize that victories in a minority subculture could not be decisive in the country as a whole. And something else was happening: their ranks were still aglow with fervor, and when Debs came to speak at Rutgers Square thousands hurried to listen, but the unions these garment workers had built were now close to stabilization, and the first signs could be noticed of that "pragmatic" accommodation to the established order which strong unions seemed to require.

From the Lower East Side to Oklahoma is an endless cultural journey, yet in those fervent years there were certain underlying similarities between the immigrant Jewish socialists and the gentile farmers flocking into the Oklahoma party. Both were poor; both felt rejected and afflicted; both were still close to the emotional ground of religious faith, which they shifted—innocently, clumsily—to their new, political faith.

Seventy years later it may stagger the imagination, but the simple fact is that in 1912 Oklahoma, Texas, Arkansas, and Louisiana gave Debs over eighty thousand votes for president, almost a tenth of the party's national total. Oklahoma had the strongest state organization in the party, and by 1914 its socialists claimed twelve thousand dues-paying members in 961 locals, with over a hundred of their people elected to local office, including six in the state legislature. There was obviously a strong populist heritage at work within this Southwestern socialism and, all through its years of strength, a populist flavor—though the Southwestern socialist leaders insisted they had gone "beyond" populism. In many respects, writes James Green in his splendid book, *Grass-Roots Socialism,*

> the southwestern Socialists looked back to the radical traditions of the nineteenth century, not just to Populist agrarianism, but further back to the natural rights philosophy articulated by Tom Paine and Thomas Jefferson. . . . [B]ehind Christian Socialism they saw the millennial theology preached by the early radical revivalists. By relating their radicalism to these native traditions, the southwesterners enhanced the appeal of what they called "scientific" socialism. . . . [T]he movement involved much more than just a political party with a particular program and philosophy. As a revivalist crusade it created a kind of religious enthusiasm. . . .[1]

The bulk of the support for the Oklahoma party came from desperate renters who had no land, and impoverished small farmers squeezed by railroads, trusts, and large competitors; but there were also pockets of industrial workers—miners and loggers—who provided strong support.

I will not enter here into the details of a deeply interesting controversy between Lawrence Goodwyn, historian of American populism, and James Green, historian of agrarian socialism, regarding the extent to which populism and socialism in the agrarian states interlaced or were distinctive. The populists, drawing their main support from small farmers, had struggled for monetary easement and antimonopoly measures that would help these farmers; the Southwestern socialists, disregarding doctrinaire

Marxists* who proposed to concern themselves only with "the agrarian proletariat," tried to develop a program helping all the

---

*There was much turmoil and confusion at socialist conventions regarding "the farm problem." Among the more rigid (and ignorant) Marxists and a few wild men from Texas (one of whom, Stanley Clark, favored the "collective ownership of the entire earth") there was resistance to the Oklahoma proposals for alleviating the lot of small farmers and landless tenants. There was, said the doctrinaire comrades, nothing distinctively *socialist* about these proposals. As for the Oklahoma socialists, they tended to be radical ultimatists in general but quite sensible when it came to their own, local issues. James Green writes: "The Debsian Socialists . . . recognized that the market system of private property in land would never allow for real equality, but that the policy of forced collectivization would deprive working farmers of their natural rights. . . . [T]hose who wanted to maintain control over the land would be allowed to do so in the socialist Commonwealth. . . ." More immediately, the Oklahoma socialists intended "to open public lands for tenant use and create worker-controlled collectives for dispossessed farmers and workers, as an alternative to isolated, inefficient small farms."[2] In short, what they were trying to do—admittedly not easy—was to find ways of satisfying, and perhaps reconciling, the interests of small farmers, landless tenants, and agricultural laborers. Party theorists, like other human beings, tended to be most high-minded when it could be at others' expense. Victor Berger, cautious enough in matters of trade-union policy, objected to the Oklahoma program at the 1912 convention because it was too populistic. He argued that there was nothing necessarily socialist in government encouragement of family farms. Perhaps not; but there was certainly something humane in such a policy. Fortunately, for the Southwestern socialists, the majority of delegates went along with the Southwestern proposals.

impoverished and exploited in the rural areas, whether small farmers, landless tenants, or day laborers.

To these people socialism meant a realization of the Christian promise, the word of Jesus given flesh. From both Christianity and socialism, they extracted a millenarian yearning reflecting the desperation of their circumstances. As one of them said, socialist doctrines "link fine with the teachings of Christ." In making this linkage, however briefly or tenuously, the Southwestern socialists created for themselves what sociologists call "a culture of respect," an inner world in which they would feel valued and could express the desires that moved them. For all their persistent suspicion of "Eastern sophisticates," these Southwesterners would do something with their movement that had its points of similarity to what the Jewish socialists were doing on the Lower East Side: bringing people together, teaching them possibilities of affirmation, helping them find their voices.

In the summer, before the crops had to be taken in, the Oklahoma socialists would hold enormous encampments, at which thousands of people would gather to listen to stirring speeches by Gene Debs, Mother Jones, and Kate Richards O'Hare. Oscar Ameringer, the leading journalist of Oklahoma socialism, has left a lovely memoir:

> These encampments . . . lineal descendants of the religious and Populist camp meetings . . . usually lasted a full week. The audience came in covered wagons from as far as seventy miles around. . . .
>
> We often arranged horseback parades through the town proper. . . . A few thousand men riding through a town of perhaps not twice that many inhabitants looked like the migration of nations. Or at least, it looked as though the social revolution were just around the corner. . . .

> On the morning of the first day a mixed chorus was organized and rehearsed in Socialist songs, usually of Populist origin, sung to familiar melodies. After singing school we conducted economic and historical lessons. . . . The instructor planted himself in the chair or store box on a raised platform, then urged the audience on the ground or pine planks to ask questions. . . .[3]

Ameringer continues with a description of how he and his three sons would give concerts of classical music, playing arrangements of Beethoven, Mozart, and Schubert for a brass quartet. "They loved it. These simple people took to good music like ducks to water. Their minds were not yet corrupted by Tin Pan Alley trash. . . ." Then would come the speeches, in good nineteenth-century American fashion, long and ornate.

To many people, including some who don't identify themselves as socialists, Southwestern socialism may still seem admirable as an expression of downtrodden people asserting their humanity—a response that is surely right. But it must also be said that Southwestern socialism didn't really offer much in the way of analyzing American society or grasping the distinctive traits of American politics. The fundamentalist cast of mind, in politics as elsewhere, can rarely accommodate the problematic or the complex.

Still more radical or perhaps more fundamentalist than the Southwesterners was that segment of the Socialist Party, mostly in the West, which sympathized with the syndicalism of the Industrial Workers of the World (IWW, or the Wobblies). Their supporters, writes James Weinstein, were

> virtually disfranchised groups—nonferrous metal miners in the remote camps of the mountain states, lumber workers of northern Louisiana and the Northwest, migratory agricultural workers, and immigrant industrial workers. [These constituents of Big Bill

> Haywood, the combative Wobbly leader] existed on the edges of society. The demands of his followers were more elemental than those of other Party members because the conditions under which they lived were more barbarous, and his hostility to reform followed largely from a belief that few reforms could affect the conditions under which the membership of the IWW existed.[4]

Addicted to a verbal violence and infantile brag that students of Western humor should not find hard to identify; superbly gifted at stirring unskilled transients but with only a small capacity for understanding the desire of the average American worker for stability; contemptuous, in the main, of politics and contemptuous, without exception, of reformers; remarkably spontaneous—indeed, elevating spontaneous combustion to a principle of social life—but really without an ideology other than some improvisations on the word "sabotage" that few people understood but which, once become a fetish, caused endless grief—this was the IWW, embodiment of a fierce yet innocent native radicalism. Little wonder that to most left-wing socialists the IWW seemed "the real thing," the revolution fleshed. Hillquit could quote from *Capital,* but Haywood looked like the specter haunting the bourgeoisie.

Yet even at the height of its success the IWW was becoming an anachronism. Immediately after its great 1912 textile strike in Lawrence, Massachusetts, the IWW had fourteen thousand members in that city; a year later only seven hundred. The Wobbly organizers, footloose, eager for new excitements, indifferent to organizational routine, had been unable to create a lasting union. For all its courage and vitality, the IWW failed to root itself in American life. It could not keep the workers it enrolled; it could not build stable industrial unions; it remained wide open to the charge—sometimes valid, sometimes not—of dual unionism; and it helped corrode the faith of the radical workers in political action, thereby dealing an unintended blow at the socialists. Failing to grasp the significance of the machine process and the modern city, the Wobblies and their friends within the Socialist Party could not see that the psychology of the small segment of American workers to which they appealed was not at all the psychology of most American workers. There was finally something tragic about this segment of American radicalism—utterly devoted, free of opportunist or authoritarian taint, authentically rebellious, American to its bones, yet destroying itself in the excesses of its zeal.

What Debs wrote in 1912 about the Wobblies was decisive: "The American workers are law-abiding and no amount of sneering . . . will alter the fact. Direct action will never appeal to any considerable number of them while they have the ballot and the right of industrial and political organization. Sabotage repels the American worker. He is ready for the industrial union but he is opposed to the 'propaganda of the deed.'"[5]

These were the main groupings within the party, reflecting the sharply different levels of development in American industrial capitalism. There were other tendencies. Christian socialists, commonly Protestant ministers and ex-ministers, spoke for a non-Marxist social gospel. (Some of the better socialist organizers were former ministers who had picked up their skills while managing congregations.) Municipal reformers found their way into the larger branches of the party. Orthodox Marxists, some of them pedants scrutinizing holy writ and others embryonic Bolsheviks, clustered in the cities. And then, I suppose, the intellectuals—except for a few, like William English Walling, not a very impressive lot—must be considered a distinct group, subject, as always in political movements, to the rank-and-file's mixture of respect and suspicion. That the socialist intellectuals were not of high quality did some harm to the party, though in a larger perspective it did not matter very much. What mattered was that American culture in these years—the muck-rakers, the Chicago Renaissance, soon *The Masses*—was buoyant, critical, energetic, a natural ally for movements of insurgency.

American socialism flourished a few decades after the time of the robber barons, the brutalities of Social Darwinism, rapid industrialization, shameless strikebreaking, labor spying. Coarsely primitive in its accumulations, early industrial capitalism could easily be taken as the enemy by everyone within, and a good many outside, the party. Victor Berger may have had little love for Big Bill Haywood, but there was still enough common hatred for the bosses, still enough class solidarity, for Berger to come to the help of Haywood's men when they took to the picket lines.

Meanwhile, the glow of Progress shone on the native horizon, and socialists basked in this glow quite as much as other Americans, only they gave it a different name. If, somehow, you managed to blend faith in Progress with a Marxist, or vulgar-Marxist, notion about "the inevitability of socialism," then you could respond to the once-famous slogan of the *Appeal to Reason*: "Socialism is not just a theory—it is a destiny." Today this may seem embarrassingly uncomplicated, but in 1912 intelligent and serious people held to it firmly. No wing of the Socialist Party thought capitalism could be reformed to any significant extent, despite the burgeoning Progressive movement, which proposed to do precisely that; and meanwhile the movement kept growing, so that despite differences over strategy that might send you into a rage with Debs or Berger or Haywood, you shared with all of them a vision of a redeemed future.

Debs's personality exerted a spell over all the comrades, including those who grumbled about his deficiencies as a leader. Read today, his speeches seem mostly wilted flowers from the garden of nineteenth-century eloquence. But everyone testified to his sincerity and goodness, a voice of fraternity that held even hostile audiences in its grip. One "hard-bitten" socialist—the story is told by Debs's biographer, Nick Salvatore—felt that a good part of socialist agitation was mere "sentimental flummery," but, he added, "the funny part of it is that when Debs says 'comrade' it is all right. He means it. That old man with the burning eyes actually believes that there can be such a thing as the brotherhood of man. And that's not the funniest part of it. As long as he's around, I believe it myself."[6]

Beset by severe inner contradictions, sometimes rhetorically indulgent and feckless, Debsian socialism must still seem—especially to those who have tasted the sour fruits of a later, ideologically "correct" radicalism—an attractive enterprise. It was a socialism generous in its sentiments, quick to offer solidarity to the oppressed: striking workers, besieged farmers, isolated miners, hungry sharecroppers. It linked immigrant laborers and native craftsmen. It brought together, as comrades no less, "Red Tom" Hickey of Texas and Meyer London of the Lower East Side. It enabled, despite residues of sexist condescension, a good number of women—Kate Richards O'Hare, Lena Morrow Lewis, Mary White Ovington, Rose Pastor Stokes—to rise to party prominence at a time when women in the United States were still fighting for the suffrage. It tolerated a wide diversity of opinion within the ranks, never lusting for the monolithism of later radical movements. It spoke—sometimes, I'll argue, almost too much—in the native idiom, the accents of American idealism.

But from a later socialist perspective, what seems most impressive about the Debsian party is that it was not a sect. Perhaps there were some sects within it, but the party had succeeded in wrenching itself out of that narrow-spirited hermeticism which marks the life of the sect. Its very faults were organically related to its virtues. Nothing is easier for the historian—say, someone like Aileen Kraditor who has made the leap from old leftist to new conservative—than to point out the frequent incoherence, the rhetorical self-indulgence, the intellectual laxities of Debsian socialism. All these were certainly present. But you cannot expect to find in a living movement the kind of ideological strictness or even moral purity you may find in a sect. Nor can you expect to find in a party of more than a hundred thousand members the intellectual refinements said to characterize elite scholarly groups. Nor should you be surprised that a movement opposing the dominant culture nevertheless takes on many of its qualities, betraying failures on issues such as racism that now shock us. A socialist movement aspires to transform human consciousness, but insofar as it embraces masses of people, it must deal with consciousness untransformed.

By 1912 the Socialist Party had reached a dangerous point. It was safely past the isolation of the sect, but not quite yet a mass movement. What it needed—and quickly—was to double its membership. The party had become large enough to be regarded as a threat by the powers-that-be (especially by Theodore Roosevelt in his antisocialist fulminations) yet not strong enough to defend itself from the attacks it would soon have to face. And its inner flaws of thought began to count more heavily, precisely insofar as the party itself did. We need look at only a few of these.

Streaks of racism besmirched the Debsian party—not as large or nasty as those in the country as a whole or even in Theodore Roosevelt's lily-white Progressivism, but visible nonetheless. Later historians would sometimes try to align positions on racism with the right-left divisions in the party, but the facts do not permit this. Victor Berger was an open racist, but so were such left-wing socialists as the editor Herman Titus and the writer Jack London. The South Carolina, Georgia, and Mississippi parties practiced segregation within their locals; the 150 black socialists in Mississippi were relegated to being members-at-large and kept out of the locals; yet there were fully integrated locals in Arkansas, Louisiana, and Kentucky. (Many Southern locals, while in accord with Victor Berger on racial issues, nevertheless voted for his left-wing opponents within the party.) The Texas socialist organization had a spotty record on racial matters; the nearby Oklahoma party a better one. Much evidently depended on the quality of local leadership. Debs and Haywood were very good on racial issues, Debs refusing to speak before segregated audiences and openly berating Southern comrades who revealed prejudice, Haywood actively promoting biracialism in the unions he led. Victor Berger, when a congressman from Wisconsin, consistently voted in behalf of black rights. The left-wing socialist intellectual William English Walling, the right-wing socialist intellectual Charles Edward Russell, and the socialist settlement-house worker Mary White Ovington were central figures in forming the NAACP. Some sections of the party had splendid records on race, especially the dockworkers of New Orleans and the miners in various states—the latter partly as a result of a tradition of equality established by the United Mine Workers.*

Not until about 1917—when A. Phillip Randolph, the black labor leader, established *The Messenger,* a socialist monthly addressed to Negroes and claiming a circulation of more than forty thousand—did the party begin paying serious attention to the blacks in America, especially that segment of the black working

---

*Race came up in another way. Convention after convention, the party kept debating the painful issue of immigration: did it favor restrictions on free entry of immigrants?

Principle required a strict internationalist stand. Experience, prejudice, and, in some instances, ties with the AFL prompted some socialists to favor limitations on immigration, especially that of Asians, who, they felt, were used as cheap labor to undermine the living standards of American workers. Here too right-left divisions within the party counted for little, since both Victor Berger and the leftist *Appeal to Reason* wanted to keep out "the yellow hordes." For the Jewish socialists the issue was especially difficult, their interest as immigrant Jews and their role as unionists coming into conflict. Meyer London, soon to be the successful socialist candidate for Congress on the Lower East Side of Manhattan, favored unrestricted immigration, thereby reflecting faithfully the sentiments of his constituency. Morris Hillquit, who believed a prime condition for building a socialist movement was to maintain good relations with the unions, took a more ambiguous position, which brought upon him harsh attacks in the Yiddish press.

As for the Socialist Party itself, it straddled the issue at its 1910 convention with a facing-two-ways resolution introduced by Hillquit. This resolution favored measures "to prevent the immigration of strikebreakers and contract laborers, and the mass importation of workers from foreign countries," whose arrival would threaten American stan-

class which was created by a mass migration northward. Yet Debsian socialism never did work out a sophisticated or even an adequate understanding of the place of blacks in American society. Because it remained captive to the simplistic notion that the only thing that finally mattered was a counterposition of socialism to capitalism, the Debsian party offered little analysis or program or even tactical help regarding "the Negro problem." On this, Debs was as thickheaded as he was pure-spirited. He kept saying that "there is no 'Negro problem' apart from the general labor problem," and that the party "had nothing specific to offer the Negro. . . . [w]e cannot make special appeals to all races."[8]

Nothing specific to offer the Negro! There could hardly be a greater admission of sectarian obtuseness. For the one thing the socialists could have offered the American black community was a fierce, unqualified struggle against Jim Crow in the here-and-now, rather than preachments about the anticipated bliss of the

---

dards of living. In the next paragraph it opposed "the exclusion of any immigrants on account of their race or nationality."

It was this sort of evasion that had led, a year earlier, the black leader W. E. B. DuBois to tell a socialist audience in New York that "the Negro race will not take kindly to Socialism so long as the international Socialist movement puts up the bars against any race whether it be yellow or black. . . . If Socialism is to gain the confidence of the Negro and get him to join the Socialist Party it will have to begin by changing its attitude toward the yellow races. . . ."[7]

From a principled socialist standpoint, Hillquit's resolution was indefensible—as he must have known. But he felt it necessary in order to keep his party together and to maintain relations with the organized working class in America. Some will condemn him; others will mutter about intolerable choices.

Cooperative Commonwealth. To collapse all problems into "the general labor problem," as Debs proposed, made for a decided economy; but also for a distinct thoughtlessness. A great deal about "the Negro problem" could not be subsumed under "the general labor problem," for racism in America had taken on a life of its own, quite as a spreading cancer takes on a life of its own. The Debsian fundamentalists, with the best will in the world, made it impossible for the socialist movement to gain deeper support among the blacks, and prevented it from apprehending many of the complexities marking American society.*

Still, should we now sit in judgment on the Debsian socialists for their flawed record on the "Negro problem"? Only if we bear in mind that in comparison with almost everyone else in American society, the socialists looked pretty good. Even Victor Berger, despite his racist bias, acted steadily in Congress to support the rights of blacks. At worst, one can say that the record of the socialists on this matter was ambivalent; about the rest of the country, alas, there is little occasion for saying as much as that.

Another problem—perhaps the crucial one—rocked the movement year after year: What attitude should socialists take toward the AFL and its moderate, even conservative leaders? Toward the anarcho-syndicalist IWW, which the AFL attacked as a dual union? Such questions were oppressively real because socialists had some influence within the unions and rightly took

*One socialist writer, I. M. Rubinow, asked a chilling question: "Are you so very sure that the Cooperative Commonwealth is unthinkable with Jim Crow cars, and other characteristic virtues of modern Southern life?"[9] The question was especially pointed in view of the Debsian tendency to envisage socialism as a society that—by definition, so to say—solves all problems.

them to be a main arena for activity. Those who were officials in the AFL felt that socialist support of the IWW would seriously hurt their standing; the small number active in the IWW felt that support of the AFL was a betrayal of the revolution. So complex are these issues, I can only try to sketch a few.

The difficulties the socialists faced vis-à-vis unionism was, above all, a reflection of the weakness of the American labor movement. Had there been a powerful trade-union federation encompassing even a large minority of the American working class, such problems would never have arisen. Once they did arise, the socialists failed to grapple with them in a sufficiently rigorous way. They failed to think through the necessary character and limitations of trade unions in a capitalist society. In 1912 the AFL, with fewer than a million members, was largely confined to skilled craftsmen, a stable work force that could use its skill monopolies to gain good contracts. The AFL made little effort to organize industrial and unskilled workers. It argued, with some plausibility and more smugness, that many of the industrial and unskilled workers were illiterate immigrants drifting from place to place, job to job, and lacking the stability that unionism required.

Now, the socialist argument for industrial unions, only two or three decades ahead of its time, was a strong one. The socialist criticism of "pure and simple" unionism—that it could not cope with problems collective bargaining did not even touch—was in principle a cogent one. But it was often pushed to such destructive extremes, with wanton denunciations of the AFL and its president, Samuel Gompers, as "reactionary," that the distance between socialists and unionists was unnecessarily widened. Debs himself was a major sinner in this respect, but even Victor Berger could denounce Gompers as "one of the most vicious and venom-ous enemies of Socialism and progressive trade unionism in America."

The historian James Weinstein writes that "Throughout his Socialist days, Debs favored the formation of a new federation of revolutionary industrial unions, believing it useless to attempt to change the AFL. . . . Any effort to influence the 'rotten graft-infected' Federation, he declared, would be 'as useless as to spray a cesspool with attar of roses.'"[10]

By its very nature, however, a trade union must primarily devote itself to limited ends. It must sign contracts in order to assure that the gains won today are honored tomorrow, and in doing this it becomes, so to speak, part of the daily functioning of capitalist society. As Bernard Shaw shrewdly if one-sidedly put it, unions are the capitalism of the workers. And the same is true for unions led by socialists and, in later decades, communists too. For if a union were to become, say, mainly an agency of revolutionary politics, it would endanger its survival as a union. When the IWW refused to sign lasting agreements ("time contracts") with employers, it was in effect committing suicide as a union. True, a "revolutionary union" may thrive briefly in an extreme or revolutionary situation, but most of the time "revolutionary unionism" tends to be a contradiction in terms. Which is not to say that unions cannot or should not complement their wage-and-hours negotiations with political activities. That, indeed, is what unions have been doing since the 1930s, when the CIO ushered in "social unionism."

Had the Debsians, as loyal though critical adherents of labor, stressed the need for industrial unionism and political involvement, while at the same time avoiding the damaging impression that they wanted to make the trade unions into a kind of socialist auxiliary, they would have made good sense and probably increased their influence. But when they attacked Gompers for "class collaboration," without recognizing that unions are inherently agencies of both "class struggle" and "class collaboration," the Debsians threatened the unity of the labor movement—a movement that included, as it had to, strongly antisocialist elements, especially large numbers of Catholics. Gompers had his own, unattractive reasons for fighting the socialists, but too many of the latter played into his hands with careless language and wanton tactics.

Relations between the moderate unionists and the socialists were exacerbated by the issue of "dual unionism." Again some elementary distinctions are needed. If an industrial union unaffiliated with the AFL, like the Amalgamated Clothing Workers, organized in an area where the AFL either had no affiliate or had only a nominal one, that hardly constituted dual unionism—even though the AFL might fling that charge at any and all unions outside its ranks. When the IWW was first set up in 1905, it seldom impinged on any workers organized by the AFL, yet by its uncompromising hostility to the AFL it came increasingly to be seen, even by its friends, as at least potentially a dual union. And by 1913 there was no question but that the IWW had begun to invade areas in which the AFL had stable affiliates—tragically, the IWW struck out against the Western Federation of Miners, a lively industrial union that had joined the IWW in 1905 but had rejoined the AFL in 1911. Thereby the IWW laid itself open to the charge both of dual unionism and of trying to undermine one of the more militant American unions. The Wobblies shrugged off such charges, but the socialists should have been troubled. Some were.

By then, however, a good part of the damage had been done. Debs joined the IWW at its opening convention, as did other socialists. Gradually, he became antagonized by the Wobblies' rhetoric of "sabotage" (of which, by the way, the loud IWW was probably less guilty than the sober AFL). Recognizing that the IWW was unable to maintain lasting unions, he quietly left it a few years later. But he still held to the chimera of setting up a rival, "revolutionary" labor federation, and thereby helped to deepen the rift between socialists and the AFL unionists.

The twists and turns of events were of course far more complicated than this sketch allows, and to help fill in the picture I give just a few details:

The socialists had considerable support within the Western Federation of Miners, especially its leadership. A small but militant union of metal miners, the Federation had its base mostly in isolated Western towns, developed a rich internal culture, and repeatedly had to conduct bitter strikes against a peculiarly vicious set of owners. In 1905 it became the largest group within the IWW—some twenty-seven thousand out of fifty thousand members—but then, because it recognized that the IWW policy of refusing to sign contracts was disastrous, it went on its own. As late as 1914 the Western Federation was conducting negotiations to unite with the AFL-affiliated United Mine Workers, and Debs, writes the labor historian John Laslett, "expressed the hope that a new industrial-union federation could be established which would draw to itself 'all the trade unions with industrial tendencies' and that the 'reactionary federation of craft unions [could] be transformed within and without into a revolutionary organization.'"[11] Again, this erratic Debsian course was damaging to socialists within the established unions.

The right-wing socialists, meanwhile, not only argued, plausibly enough, that it was necessary to work within the AFL; but, in part because they had begun to find comfort in their leadership positions and in part because they were reacting defensively to charges of "opportunism," they also gradually abandoned or softened their criticisms of the Gompers leadership. There really was no good reason to do this, except for the familiar law that one excess provokes another.

Clearly the task of American socialists in relation to unionism was far more complicated than that of European socialists, who enjoyed close relations with, or leadership within, the unions. This was itself a major sign of the larger difficulties socialists faced in America, and if they couldn't find a way to at least moderately cordial relations with the major unions, then they probably could not find a way toward establishing themselves as a major force in the country.

In principle the outline of an appropriate policy vis-à-vis the unions was available to the socialists. It was declared by some of them: to recognize the dominant status of the AFL and the legitimacy of its stress on collective bargaining, while criticizing in fraternal fashion its failure to organize the mass of industrial workers; to distinguish clearly between the functions of unions and the Socialist Party; to support particular IWW strikes where workers were struggling for better conditions but to avoid any impression of endorsing the IWW's tilt toward dual unionism or its fantasy about "revolutionary unionism"; and to stress the value, in the American setting, of political activity against the syndicalism of the Wobblies. These are elements of a formula, and formulas can never cope with a reality so chaotic and contradictory as the condition of American labor in those years. Morris Hillquit came closest to speaking for this outlook. So did Debs at times, but erratically and with damaging lapses into the rhetoric of "revolutionary unionism." Debs's language was a good deal more "revolutionary" than his practice—which meant that neither a consistently reformist nor consistently revolutionary course was taken.

In 1904 there occurred a fascinating colloquy between the socialist Morris Hillquit and Samuel Gompers, head of the AFL. The latter explained that the goal of trade unionists was "to accomplish the best results in improving the conditions of the working people . . . today and tomorrow and tomorrow—and tomorrow's tomorrow. . . ." There followed this exchange:

> H.: Now, my question is, Will this effort on the part of organized labor ever stop until it has the full reward for its labor?
>
> G.: It won't stop at all.
>
> H.: Then, the object of the labor union is to obtain complete social justice for themselves . . . ?
>
> G.: It is the effort to obtain a better life every day.
>
> H.: Every day and always—
>
> G.: Every day. That does not limit it.
>
> H.: Until such time—
>
> G.: Not until any time.
>
> H.: In other words—
>
> G.: In other words we go further than you. You have an end; we have not.[12]

Probably unawares, Gompers was here linking, in our characteristic fashion, American "pragmatism" with American "idealism," the day-to-day immediate demands with an endless vista of improvement. Hillquit should have had no difficulty in replying that Gompers was playing games with the word "end." He, Hillquit, thought of socialism as an end in the sense of a goal, not a termination, so that the Gompersian vista did not really exclude socialism as a major step along a sequence of steps without necessary end.

The difference between Hillquit and Gompers was, of course, large and real. But I don't think it a sign of caving in before "the labor bureaucracy" to suggest that if the Debsian socialists hadn't been so infatuated with their "revolutionary" language and had followed the more considered if less dramatic approach of Hillquit, there might have resulted, not complete harmony, but at least a better relationship between socialists and unionists. How much difference that would finally have made to the outcome of American socialism we cannot say; but if *anything* in the earlier decades of the century might have made a difference, it would have been this.

Daniel Bell has an interesting passage which follows the lines of this discussion:

> To the socialists the demand for a shorter work-day and more wages was no solution to the capitalist crisis. Some ultimate goal had to be fixed lest the workers gain illusions that the trade union was a sufficient instrument for melioration. If one accepts the viewpoint that a union, by its own nature, becomes an end in itself and an integral part of capitalist society, then such a socialist theory makes sense. If, however, one regards unionism as a social force which by its own position in an industrial hierarchy becomes a challenge to managerial power and changes the locus of power in capitalism, then Gompers' strategy of focusing on the day-to-day issues was undeniably correct.[13]

Undeniably correct, I'd say, *for the unions.* That the accumulation of daily gains might also humanize and modulate capitalist society in a sort of American adaptation of social democracy, was a consideration few Debsians were prepared to take seriously or find attractive. They suffered, as I shall argue, from a simplistic notion of capitalism-or-socialism and took no serious interest in intermediary or mixed states. What mattered at the time, however, was to keep a clear distinction between the ends of a union and the ends of the party; and this, to their own political cost, the Debsians did not always do.

Debsian socialism verged at times on the nebulous, at times on the evangelical, at times on the sectarian; but what brought many people into the movement was a shared desire for a deep-going revaluation of values. Thousands of Americans became socialists out of an impulse toward moral generosity, a readiness to stake their hopes on some goal beyond personal success. As Nick Salvatore writes in his biography of Debs:

> The religious tone that permeated this Socialist movement did not negate the growing class awareness—but it did interpret that consciousness in a particular cultural context. The crisis in people's lives, as in their society, was no mere intellectual problem. Rather, as H. Richard Niebuhr has suggested, it fostered a "revolutionary temper" and a belief that "life is a critical affair" and forced each to confront the "necessity of facing the ultimate realities of life. . . ." This convergence of religious and secular millenarianism generated a powerful social critique. A common religious impulse provided moral principles—the notion of "right"—to denounce capitalism; the democratic tradition provided the context through which class anger found expression; and deteriorating social conditions supplied the impetus for anger and action.[14]

By now it is hard not to conclude that this socialism also contained too large a quota of innocence, too great a readiness (which put it quite in the American grain) to let spirit do the work of mind. The vision of the future held by most of these socialists was remarkably unproblematic. Questions that have since troubled people on the left—the relation between workers and the party speaking in their name, the difficulties of aligning economic planning with personal freedom, the specter of bureaucratism—were seldom discussed during the Debsian era, and then only by a few intellectuals. Like most Americans of their day, the Debsians had little talent for self-doubt; like most Americans, they worked for a gleaming future with the assurance of people who have not yet heard our century's bad news.

Behind such attitudes lay a strong sentiment of evangelicism. Anyone who reads E. P. Thompson's account of English evangelical radicalism in *The Making of the English Working Class* will recognize similar, perhaps derived, elements of belief and feeling in the American radical experience. An American who has shared the life of our radical movements is likely to nod in recognition when Thompson writes that "the Methodist political rebel carried through into his radical or revolutionary activity a profound moral earnestness, a sense of righteousness and of 'calling,' a 'Methodist' capacity for sustained organizational dedication and (at its best) a high degree of personal responsibility."[15] In later years American socialists might speak in the phrases of Marxism, but anyone with an ear for the native accent could detect a deeper note—the preacher's call to salvation, the Emersonian prod to self-fulfillment.

If this quasi-religious fervor gave Debsian socialism energy, purity, and goodness, it also made for less attractive qualities. Debsian socialism carried within itself a dybbuk of sectarianism that damaged the movement even in its best years; and that sectarianism, profoundly native in flavor, had a major source, I believe, in the many branches of American Protestantism. The tradition of moral testimony, sometimes moral absolutism—with its tendency to reduce human existence to blunt compartments of good and evil, its frequent readiness to set the claims of conscience above the bonds of community—could turn out to be in deep tension with a democratic polity requiring compromise and entailing imperfection. The tradition of moral testimony could inspire great social movements, most notably abolitionism; it served protest along the rim of political life better than parties squarely within that life; but a quantity of mischief could easily be made by groups like the Debsian party when they teetered uneasily, ambivalently, between moral protest and political action.

The evangelical note was not, of course, the only one to be heard. In cities where the socialists won municipal elections—Milwaukee, Berkeley, Schenectady—the party settled into mild reform. Among Jewish garment workers it slowly melded with the "social unionism" of the ILGWU and the ACWA. Yes, Debsian socialism remained a "coalition party"—that is, a party that was itself a coalition—but the dominant voice, especially in national electoral campaigns, was that of Debs.

At first his soaring evangelicism was enormously enabling for the party, but later it became seriously disabling. It formed the cultural basis, I think, for the simple dualism to which the Debsians clung, the notion that there were two, and only two, choices facing mankind: capitalism (the devil's spawn) and socialism (the angelic promise). Only a few socialist intellectuals, like William English Walling, glimpsed the possibility that there might be multiple courses in modern history—that the trend toward statification of the economy might lead to a bastard formation called "state capitalism," or that there might occur a gradual transition toward a "welfare state" or "mixed economy." Such ideas, if mooted at the time, were anathema to the Debsians. This did not matter very much as long as American capitalism clung to a brutal spirit of domination unwilling to make concessions to plebeian and labor needs. But once the American political elite grew more sophisticated—and this was how William English Walling explained the rise of Progressivism—then the Debsian approach ran into trouble.

You could see this trouble in the narrow Debsian approach to "the Negro problem," in its damaging oscillations of attitude toward the labor unions, in its refusal or inability to recognize the growing complication and sophistication of capitalism, and in its almost religious belief that socialists should never vote for anyone, no matter how liberal, who ran for office on an old-party ticket.*

When I first began to examine this dogma critically, it seemed like a baneful inheritance from Bolshevism. But I have come to believe that it is really, or also, an inheritance of Debsianism, handed down by the leaders of an indigenous movement for whom an electoral bloc with liberals seemed as sinful as dealing with agents of the devil had seemed to their grandparents.

If I am right, then we ought to qualify, though not deny, the

---

*I can testify to the power this belief held over people on the left even in later years. To vote for Norman Thomas, during the years of my socialist youth, seemed akin to being flooded with grace—or at least sprinkled. Even after many of us had decided that running socialist candidates once there was barely a socialist movement had become a humiliating ritual, and that it was necessary to vote for "the lesser of the two evils" when there was one—even then it was still emotionally hard to go to the polls and pull down an old-party lever. The first time I did that, voting in 1952 for Adlai Stevenson, I came out of the voting booth feeling almost physically sick.

thesis of "American exceptionalism"—the thesis that concludes that conditions in this country require major adaptations of socialist politics, approach, and voice. For precisely insofar as the Debsians were rooted in the traditions of their culture, they were kept from seeing that their fundamentalist socialism was becoming increasingly ill-adapted to a rapidly changing American society. It was the immigrant German Victor Berger, and the immigrant Jew Morris Hillquit, who, approaching American society from a certain distance, now and then showed a keener grasp of its political styles and possibilities than the native Debsians. At the party's 1912 convention the forces represented by Hillquit and Berger had pushed through a clause mandating the expulsion of any member advocating "sabotage"—a thrust at Haywood and the Wobblies, which indicated an understanding that in America a party wishing to be more than a sect would have to work within the confines of republican legitimacy. But what the socialists could not cope with was the interplay between two American traditions: the one that made "playing by the rules" of democracy an all-but-universal credo, and the one that inspired so many of the comrades to a quasi-religious radical fervor. The faith inspiring the ranks braked the party.

I am saying something rather different here from what Daniel Bell has said in his influential history of American socialism. He writes: "The socialist movement, by its very statement of goals and its rejection of the capitalist order as a whole, could not relate itself to the specific problems of the here-and-now, give-and-take political world. It was trapped by the unhappy problem of living '*in* but not *of* the world.'"[16]

Bell is clearly on to something, as must be evident to anyone who looks back to the founding 1901 convention of the party, where an "impossibilist" wing fought against advocating any "immediate demands." This group was defeated, though not until

Hillquit fretted publicly that if it won, "other parties will stand for progress and we for dreams." But Bell's formula has only a limited value, for at least three reasons. First, socialists, if they are to remain socialists, must in part not be "of the world" even as they must also work within it. Otherwise, they give up the idea of historical transcendence, the vision of *another* society. In his resort to Max Weber's counterposition between the "ethic of responsibility" and the "ethic of conscience" Bell comes down too heavily—so it must seem from a socialist point of view—in behalf of the "ethic of responsibility." He tends to forget what socialists, by their very vocation, must remember: that Weber also wrote, "Certainly all historical experience confirms the truth —that man would not have attained the possible unless time and again he had reached out for the impossible." Second, there is no reason in principle why advocacy of a basic transformation of society should keep a party from being able to "relate itself to the . . . here-and-now, give-and-take political world"—though linkage between the two can in practice cause severe tensions. And third, Bell's formula seems timeless and placeless, indeed world-encompassing, so that it would presumably apply to Europeans as well as Americans—which is to say, it doesn't much help to explain the sharply different fates of the American and European parties.

No, the trouble with Debsian socialism was not primarily that it was "*in* but not *of* the world," nor that a part of its "soul" resisted the enticements of the historical given. The trouble was its failure adequately to grasp, and relate to, the changing nature of "the world" as it was, once America had passed the formative time of industrial capitalism.

The decline of the Debsian party was rapid: from 1912 to 1917. Daniel Bell argues that it was mainly due to the right-left intraparty dispute of 1912, James Weinstein that the party didn't really suffer serious losses until the government began its repression after the United States entered World War I. It is hard to decide, and the reason is that so little time elapsed between one supposed cause of decline and another. Let me sketch out the sequence: 1912, the "antisabotage" clause in the Socialist program leads to the departure from the party of the leftist, pro-Wobbly elements, mostly in the West, at about the time that Wilsonian Progressivism is drawing away members from the right wing of the movement; but only a few years intervene between these events and the American entry into the war, the Socialist Party's opposition to which must soon evoke governmental reprisals; yet only a few months later comes the 1917 Bolshevik Revolution, which tears apart the world-wide socialist movement and leads to the establishment of the Communist International. These events cascade so rapidly, it seems best to take them in sequence, without pretending to certainty about their respective weights.

Woodrow Wilson's first administration introduced significant new social legislation anticipating the "welfare state" of Franklin Roosevelt's New Deal. A graduated income tax, the Clayton Act to limit labor injunctions, a child-labor law, several laws helping farmers, the direct election of senators—these and other reforms, part of the traditional socialist legislative program, were rapidly enacted. The Progressives were neither entirely consistent nor entirely progressive. There was a strong elitist component in the Progressivist outlook; its record on Negro enfranchisement was bad, and the unions had grounds to complain about the Wilson administration. Nevertheless, a major shift of national policy had begun away from laissez-faire policies. There lay behind Progressivism an impatience with "the energetic and selfish individualism" that its spokesman Herbert Croly saw as part of the

Jeffersonian tradition; a belief in the need for a strong, reforming central government; a commitment to social amelioration that would right the imbalances cast up by unregenerate capitalism without, however, threatening its fundamental relations of power.

Leading left-wing intellectuals, from Max Eastman to A. M. Simons and even John Reed, supported Wilson in the 1916 election; a number of trade unions previously close to the socialists started edging over toward Wilson. Socialist losses in membership seem mainly to have been due to resignations of pro-Wobbly leftist members; their losses in votes, to the pull of Progressivism. The socialists did poorly in 1916, partly because an ailing Debs did not run but also because the process had begun through which old-party liberal candidates undermine socialist strength by appropriating some of their immediate proposals.

For the socialists this was a disorienting experience. They might have learned from similar "interventionist" policies undertaken in Europe by Bismarck and Lloyd George; but only a few of them did. Their response to this problem, as to many others, did not, however, follow any clear left-right division. There were left-wing Socialists, like the Debsian cohort, who behaved as if they needed only to repeat the usual fundamental, or fundamentalist, attack on capitalism, arguing that the Wilsonian reforms were largely cosmetic; but there were also left-wing socialists, like the editors of the *International Socialist Review,* who provided a somewhat more complex analysis, seeing Progressivism as the American businessman's discovery "that he can carry on certain portions of the productive process more efficiently through *his* government than through private corporations." William English Walling published in 1914 a book called *Progressivism and After* in which he offered a sophisticated argument that the "individualism" Theodore Roosevelt and Woodrow Wilson hoped to preserve—that is, "the system of competition . . . by private capital" —could now be saved "only by ceding a large part of the field to collectivism."[17] Walling argued that collectivism was not necessarily socialist; indeed, there were "state-capitalist" forms on the historical agenda that, for good or bad, Progressivism was going to introduce. By contrast, the usually flexible Hillquit did not quite grasp the meaning of this new Progressivism, perhaps because he still held to a version of Marxism.

The socialist movement did not respond to Progressivism with enough flexibility in either analysis or tactics, thereby anticipating the more serious problems it would face under Franklin Roosevelt's New Deal. I take this to be a classical instance where the pragmatism upon which Americans like to praise themselves turned out to be impractical, or, put another way, where the failure to engage in serious theoretical analysis of the development of capitalism caused the socialists trouble in their day-to-day work. For it soon became clear that Progressivism, especially when spoken for by an attractive leader like Robert La Follette, was going to be a serious competitor to the socialists, and that neither tub-thumping invective nor impatient dismissals would dispose of this competition.*

---

*These issues were raised in a sharp and interesting way by the young Walter Lippmann in 1913, after he had resigned his post as secretary to the newly elected socialist mayor of Schenectady. Lippmann, then going through the leftist phase that in America often precedes becoming an Establishment spokesman, wrote a long letter to the socialist national office arguing that the socialist fear of antagonizing "the property-holders whose votes decided the election" kept the new administration from raising the tax rate. But, argued Lippmann, the rate had to be increased so that the "Socialist administration [could] cut into

Still, one can think of an excuse or two for the socialist failure to respond adequately to this new political situation—after all, no one ever responds quickly enough to new political situations, and the socialists had little time in which to work out a considered view of Progressivism. Soon after the start of Wilson's second term, the country entered the war, and the troubles caused by Progressivism were dwarfed by far greater ones.

The stand the American socialists took toward World War I became for them a testing of spirit and an assertion of virtue. In the mythology of the American left—I use that phrase in no disparaging way—the party's opposition to the war came to acquire an aura of heroism. For the Debsians it was a crucial instance of standing up to that damned Wall Street government, quite as Thoreau had denounced the Mexican War. For the Marxists, even moderate ones like Hillquit, it was a reassertion of principle, though privately Victor Berger feared it was also a reckless gesture.

---

the returns of property, [in order] to take as much of them as possible to be spent for social purposes." The basic difficulty, said Lippmann, was that "We [socialists] try to do the things that reformers can do at least as well as we, and we try to represent at the same time a profoundly revolutionary movement. Supermen might do it. We can't." What Lippmann then proposed was that socialists advance only those reforms too radical for the Progressives to accept, thereby drawing a clear line of distinction—"That is the way to keep the progressives from voting our ticket."[18]

Lippmann's analysis was keen, but his proposals utterly sectarian, implying a kind of purity that could only isolate socialists from potential allies. A sensible, though not easy, solution to the problems he posed would have been to keep raising the ante, moving ahead from reform to reform, immediate demand to demand.

A few days after the declaration of war, the socialists convened in St. Louis and by an overwhelming majority denounced America's entry as "a crime against the people," declared it a war imperialistic on both sides, and pledged that "in support of capitalism, we will not willingly give a single life or a single dollar." It called upon party members to engage in "continuous, active and public opposition" to conscription, and to offer "vigorous resistance" to assaults on liberties or the right to strike. Small and vulnerable, the socialist movement in America stood proudly by the traditional antiwar position of the Socialist International, which most of its powerful European members had abandoned.

Did the socialists have any idea of the price they would have to pay for their antiwar stand? Did they anticipate that it would cause or lead to the jailing of their leaders, the destruction of a third of their locals, and the banning from the mails of most of their publications? Did they understand that in behalf of principle they were in effect enabling the destruction of their own party? There is no clear evidence on this matter, but I venture a speculation. The Debsian leaders were the most extreme in their denunciation of capitalist "slavery" in America, yet I suspect that in their heart of hearts they were persuaded that as free-born Americans they possessed inalienable rights, perhaps the most precious of which was to denounce the government, and that this government would not dare resort to brutal repression against free-born Americans. Leaders like Hillquit and Berger, being more temperate in language and a good deal more skeptical about American pretensions, knew that troubles lay ahead.

The immediate losses caused by the party's antiwar stand were small in number but large in consequence. Almost its entire intellectual contingent, ranging from right to left and including such figures as John Spargo, W. J. Ghent, Charles Edward Russell, A. M. Simons, Upton Sinclair, and William English Walling, resigned to support Wilson's war effort. In some instances they turned upon their former comrades with that venom which often seems a specialty of ex-radicals. In the short run, the party managed quite well without these figures; in the long run, not. Most of the socialist intellectuals of that moment strike me, perhaps unfairly, as somewhat mediocre; but at least they formed a countervoice to the tendency favoring "proletarian" fundamentalism. To be deprived of its intelligentsia, whether distinguished or pedestrian, must always be a major blow for a socialist movement.

For perhaps half a year the party gained members as a result of its antiwar stand. Thousands flocked in during 1917, the foreign-language federations swelling especially because of immigrant enthusiasm for the Russian Revolution. Only a few intellectuals opposed the war, first of all Randolph Bourne, who, while not a doctrinal socialist, shared the party's judgment that, as he wrote, it was "a hateful and futile war" which would endanger "democratic values at home." In the 1917 local elections the socialist vote zoomed dramatically, reaching an average of 22 percent—which, calculated Paul Douglas, would have meant four million votes if there had been a national election. In New York, Hillquit ran a spectacular campaign for mayor, receiving almost 22 percent of the vote. This was probably the high point of American left-wing strength, a vast outpouring of enthusiasm, tremendous mass meetings, and bitter conflicts with opponents, climaxed by Theodore Roosevelt's attack on Hillquit as "yellow calls to yellow." The 1917 socialist vote was high: in New York 22 percent, Chicago 34 percent, Dayton 44 percent, Toledo 34 percent, Cleveland 19 percent.

It isn't hard to see why socialist leaders should have felt optimistic after such a vote; but from the convenience of historical retrospect, it is hard to understand why they didn't grasp the magnitude of the government assault soon to be directed against them. The party had taken an intransigent stand in opposition to the war, a stand that many Americans saw as "revolutionary"—though, in truth, very little about the Socialist Party was revolutionary. It lacked the toughness, perhaps the caution, which a party fundamentally opposed to the *status quo* must have, especially during wartime.

The severe Wilsonian repressions form a blot on American history, matched by outbursts of mob violence which they probably helped set off. Physical attacks upon radicals and pacifists began soon after the declaration of war. With the passage of the Espionage Act of 1917—a legislative net wide enough to catch any fish, from Wobbly sharks to pacifist minnows—the repressions became explicit policy. By the end of 1917 almost every socialist publication was banned from the mails. Party headquarters in Indiana and Ohio were raided, the national office in Chicago was occupied for three days by government agents, a convention of the South Dakota party was broken up by force, the Rand School, a socialist educational society, was fined three thousand dollars for publishing a pamphlet by Scott Nearing, and in Boston mobs of soldiers stormed the party office. The IWW suffered a good deal more, its supporters in the Southwest and West being tarred and feathered, beaten, jailed, dumped without food or water in the desert, and arrested in large numbers on charges of violating the Espionage Act.*

Before the end of the war almost every socialist leader would be prosecuted under the Espionage Act: Victor Berger, Kate Richards O'Hare, Adolph Germer (the national secretary), Charles Ruthenberg, and, of course Gene Debs. Only Hillquit, stricken with tuberculosis, was spared. For a while, reeling under

---

*The most tragic story of war resistance and government repression was set in Oklahoma. The leftist Oklahoma Socialists had unanimously

governmental attack and with some leaders coming to think that the revolution in Russia should prompt a changed attitude to-

---

adopted in December 1914 a resolution stating that "If War is declared, the Socialists of Oklahoma shall refuse to enlist; but if forced to enter military service to murder fellow workers, we shall choose to die fighting the enemies of humanity in our ranks rather than to perish fighting our fellow workers." James Green, the historian of Southwestern socialism, comments that "This 'revolutionary stand,' widely interpreted as a pledge by Socialists to 'turn their guns on their officers,' may have been 'the most disastrous ever made by the party in Oklahoma.'"

By the time of America's entry into the war, there were several thousand Oklahoma poor farmers, almost entirely native Americans, who were so bitterly opposed to entering the war that they regarded the socialist position as too tame. They organized themselves into secret societies, one of them called the Working Class Union. A smaller one, called the Jones Family, in August 1917 gathered about a thousand people in eastern Oklahoma to engage in armed resistance. Expecting similar insurrectionary moves to occur elsewhere in the Southwest, they were sadly disappointed upon discovering their isolation. One participant in what later came to be called the Green Corn Rebellion explained their motives: "We decided we wasn't gonna fight somebody else's war for 'em and we refused to go. We didn't volunteer and we didn't answer the draft."[19]

An armed posse was formed to put down the rebels; several were killed in a few skirmishes and more wounded; hundreds were arrested; and many others, numbering apparently a few thousand, fled to nearby hills, fearful for their safety. Although the Socialist Party of Oklahoma had steadily opposed violent methods and not one socialist official was involved in the Green Corn Rebellion, the Oklahoma socialists were harassed and arrested. The once-strong party structure was crushed, and an emergency convention voted to disband the Oklahoma party. Never again would socialism regain its strength in that part of the country.

ward the war, the socialists began to modulate their public views. Perhaps in response to what he saw as this "backsliding," Debs made his famous speech at Canton, Ohio, in the spring of 1918 reaffirming the St. Louis antiwar declaration. Convicted of violating the Espionage Act, he was sentenced to ten years in prison. In court Debs spoke the words that summed up the meaning of his life:

> Your Honor, years ago I recognized my kinship with all living beings, and I made up my mind that I was not one whit better than the meanest on earth. I said then, and I say now, that while there is a lower class I am in it, while there is a criminal element I am of it, and while there is a soul in prison I am not free.

It's not, I think, a mere spirit of negation that leads me, directly after these stirring words of Eugene Victor Debs, to raise the question of how wise it was for the American socialists to make their antiwar position into so intransigent—indeed, defiant—a position. My own belief is that the war, as the socialists said, was largely imperialist in character; that ordinary people had little if any stake in joining the mass slaughter in Europe; and that the United States should have been proposing, as, again, the socialists said, a peace conference to end the war. And of course it's only if one shares these opinions that it makes sense to speak of the socialist response to the war as having a "tragic" component.

Politically, the lesson of it all is that a nonrevolutionary movement cannot afford the indulgence of revolutionary postures: it loses out as a party of reform, it proves itself ineffectual as a voice of revolution. Something of the kind happened to the American socialists during World War I. But was opposition to the war necessarily a sign of revolutionary politics? Not at all—except that, with the Debsian socialists' habit of draping a fierce rhetoric onto a somewhat less-than-fierce politics, what they said *seemed* revolutionary to many Americans during a time of inflamed national feelings, and this, in turn, enabled equally inflamed authorities to pretend that it was.

As it turned out, the Socialist Party was pathetically vulnerable to government assault. The socialists had not taken the precautions that a revolutionary movement customarily takes when it anticipates repression; they hardly knew what those precautions might be.

The antiwar socialists were caught in a conflict, perhaps beyond mediation, between two positive values: to speak their truth or to protect the movement without which they could not effectively speak their truth. Had they been fully aware of the trap in which they found themselves or into which they had helped to put themselves, then their dilemma would have been genuinely "tragic." But whether many of their leading figures really grasped that they had to choose between the idea to which they were committed and the vehicle they had so laboriously constructed for realizing that idea, I find it very hard to say. Knowing the difficulties of building a socialist movement in America, I cannot bring myself simply to declare, in grand Debsian style: Let the devil do his damnedest, we will speak out in full voice. For the devil did—and the socialists paid a heavy price. Yet I also see the force of the opposing argument, that to have abandoned principle would have made the organization into an agency preserved after its purpose had been denied.

Was this conflict between the claims of public testimony and the claims of survival inescapable? Might it have been modulated or finessed a little? Would it have been better for the party to be less brave and more clever? To wriggle a little but keep itself from being all but destroyed? One historian of American socialism thinks so:

> The choice [for American socialists] was not simply between blind acceptance and blind opposition to war. Another path was open: the party's consideration of American public opinion (by which it would remain part of American society) and working for the maintenance . . . of democracy within a nation at war. . . . The overwhelming majority of voters could never regard the party sympathetically after its war stance.[20]

This formula—admittedly weak in heroics (some would say, in heroism)—is not likely to have satisfied either extreme within socialist opinion. Nor thrill the hearts of those for whom politics is mainly gesture and declamation of rectitude. But it is just possible that such a prudent course might have saved the socialist movement and enabled it to fight another day. No one can say this with certainty, and I feel somewhat uneasy, as if betraying a received piety, even to suggest it. But I have come to believe that it is right.

The rest is devastation. Despite losses to Progressivism and blows from the government, the Socialist Party kept growing during the war years. By 1919 it again had over a hundred thousand members, and this provides some comfort for those historians who believe that the leftward turn within the movement in response to the Russian Revolution was desirable. But examine the membership figures and the result seems less happy. About fifteen hundred party locals, mainly in the West, had been destroyed by wartime repressions, with major losses in native-born membership. There had been an unmeasured but significant loss along the right wing of the party. "In 1908 the foreign-born percentage of SP membership was 29% and by 1912 it was below 15%. During the war years the trend was reversed. By the end of 1915 the party was 32.5% foreign-born."[21] By 1919 over 53 percent of the members belonged to foreign-language federations.

This mattered, not because there was any inherent virtue in native birth, but because the bulk of these new foreign-language members belonging to the five Slavic federations and, constituting 30 percent of the total party membership, had joined mostly out of a sudden enthusiasm for the Russian Revolution. They cared little and knew less about the conditions of American life. They were impatient—indeed, scornful—of American socialists like Dan Hogan of Arkansas, who in 1919 said that, while all socialists gave "unqualified support to Soviet Russia," still, "the psychology of American workers is different than that of Russian workers" and socialists "must not appear to support Russian methods for America" since to do so "would isolate us."[22] The foreign-language recruits, politically raw but inflamed with passion for the new Leninist regime, were often intent upon splitting the party in order to set up a new, Communist Party in accord with the strategy of Moscow.

Nothing in the immediate prospects or inner dynamic of the American left made this split necessary. American socialism, under the quickening impact of the Russian Revolution, had already turned sharply leftward. Morris Hillquit, when arguing against a protocommunist group within the party, failed to attack the fundamental premises of Leninism (as he would a few years later) and instead argued mainly on a tactical level, i.e., refused to accept the communists' dogma that a revolutionary situation was impending in the United States and that "underground" methods of work were necessary. Even after the split in 1919, which begins the tragicomic history of American communism, the Socialist Party was still so much under the spell of the Russian Revolution (as were many other Americans) that it voted in referendum to apply for membership in the Communist International. Moscow brusquely refused—which, from all points of view, was surely to the good.

What now remained of the socialist movement was a pitiful remnant. Not only had a large minority of the party quit to begin the Katzenjammer intrigues of the communist factions, but thousands of the faithful dropped out in weariness and disgust. The golden age of American socialism—as, alas, we must still consider it—was over. Political competition from the Progressives, severe wartime repression, infatuation with the new wave of communism: one cause of decline led so quickly into another that, finally, it is almost impossible to distinguish among them or measure their respective impacts. Yet a thread of continuity can be found in the rise and fall of the American socialist movement: it would repeat itself, with variations, in the thirties and once again in the sixties. It is a thread of failure to recognize the distinctive characteristics of American life and society, complicated by an equally damaging incapacity, or refusal, to recognize that a strong native tradition of sectarianism contributes heavily to this failure.

Socialists in the Thirties

In the whole sad history of the American left, a special place must be reserved for the socialists of the thirties. For a few years, between 1931 and 1935, they seemed on the verge of becoming a vital movement. A good many people felt that the Socialist Party and its leader, the radiant and selfless Norman Thomas, might provide an answer—at once radical and democratic—to the Depression. Yet by about 1937 the party had collapsed, a victim of both severe external pressures and an inner quarrelsomeness that can't easily be distinguished from a drive to self-destruction.

When Clarence Senior, an intelligent twenty-six-year-old Missourian, became national secretary of the Socialist Party in 1929, he found the barest shell of an organization. The once-thriving party of Debs was reduced to a mere six thousand members "on the books" (which sometimes meant, nowhere else), and most of these were immigrant workers belonging to the "foreign-language federations." Only a few hundred members spoke English; when Senior reorganized the Cleveland branch in 1927, he had all of two comrades who could speak the language.

Senior's predecessor as national secretary, William H. Henry, was an old Debsian loyalist from Indiana, provincial, bumbling, half literate—one of those figures from the Midwest who might have stepped out of a Dreiser novel depicting the struggle of small-town Americans for the rudiments of culture. That the party could find no one better to run its day-to-day affairs tells almost everything about its decline. By the late 1920s it had only two centers of modest strength: Wisconsin, where descendants of German socialist settlers kept alive a municipal socialism, and New York, where the Jewish garment unions and the Yiddish *Daily Forward* provided some financial and political support. The New York socialists, consisting mainly of a few hundred veterans, called the Old Guard, were led by Morris Hillquit, a man of intellectual and personal distinction.

Brought to New York for conversations with the party leaders, Senior protested that he knew little about socialist thought. Replied Hillquit: "You've read Comrade [Harry] Laidler's book, haven't you?" Yes, he had. Continued Laidler: "You've read Comrade Hillquit's book, haven't you?" Yes, that too. "What more," concluded Hillquit (we may imagine with a touch of irony), "do you need to know about socialist theory?"[1]

Hillquit was frank about the party's condition, admitting that, at best, it came to fitful life in a few cities during electoral campaigns and then lapsed back into slumber. Somewhat later he said to Senior: "You'll have to remember that the comrades in New York have elevated inaction into a theory."[2] Competing leftists often called the Socialist Party "a retirement home."

Another young socialist of the time, Gus Tyler, has described the party headquarters in the Williamsburg district of Brooklyn, in those years heavily Jewish and very poor. The party had its offices on one floor, where old-timers would gather to play pinochle in the evenings, while in the basement there was a billiard parlor, which brought in enough income to pay the upkeep. Once Tyler visited the young socialist group that met there on Sunday afternoons and, in a plea for some activity, sarcastically remarked that the group was called the Young People's Socialist—not Social—League. His remarks were regarded as somewhat extreme.

The "tired radicals" of the Old Guard had, in their youth, been activists for Debs; they had stood fast behind the party's antiwar position during World War I; they had struggled to keep the garment unions afloat during the difficult twenties; they had fought bitterly to keep those unions out of communist hands; and they had run electoral campaigns, of a sort, all through these lean years. There were good reasons to be tired.

In part because Norman Thomas brought a new luster to the movement and Clarence Senior carefully tended a new local here and there, the party started showing signs of life. In the late twenties a number of ministers, drawn by the example of ex-minister Thomas, became active figures. Young people joined by the hundreds. Militant trade unionists, the most notable being the Reuther brothers in Detroit, enlisted in the party. In 1930 Louis Waldman, socialist candidate for governor of New York, polled over 120,000 votes, and Upton Sinclair, candidate for governor of California, over fifty thousand. But the party itself grew only modestly, certainly not so much as one might expect during a depression. Millions of Americans, even if jobless, kept hoping their troubles were only a brief interruption of American well-being. There were strikes and demonstrations of the unemployed toward the end of the Hoover administration, but these were usually sporadic and defensive in character. People had to learn through hard experience that the mood of the 1920s no longer corresponded to social reality.

During 1931, ninety-six new socialist locals were set up; in the first four months of 1932, 113 new locals. In December 1931 two young unemployed members, Amicus Most and Murray Baron, spent a month in West Virginia on the grand budget of $235, touring the state to organize several new locals. The indefatigable Norman Thomas seemed to be everywhere, speaking for strikers, fighting for civil liberties, visiting campuses to rouse young people.

I first heard Thomas speak in 1934, at a time when young people had begun to fear the Depression was no mere aberration but signaled a deep social sickness. Hearing Thomas made me suppose that some new force had entered my life, a possibility that I might now understand the ugliness and chaos everywhere about me and that perhaps I might even do a little toward a remedy.

In 1932, the party had put on the largest presidential campaign since the days of Debs. Forty full-time unpaid organizers took to the field. Ten thousand people came to hear Thomas in Indianapolis, a still greater number in Philadelphia, and at the closing rally in Madison Square Garden there were twenty-two thousand. In the end, however, Thomas polled only 903,286 votes, three times more than his 1928 count but still disappointing to his supporters. A respected newspaperman, Paul Y. Anderson of the *St. Louis Post-Dispatch,* wrote that Thomas had really gotten about two million votes, but through thievery and neglect had been denied half of them. Harry Fleischman, a socialist leader, tells a story, not at all unusual, about serving as poll watcher in a Bronx district. When the votes were counted, there were six for the Communist Party, and since no communist watcher was present, the Republican and Democratic local agents proposed that the six votes be split equally among the three parties. Good democrat that he was, Fleischman indignantly refused. Later it occurred to him that if he hadn't been there the socialist vote might also have been "redistributed."

Many people at Thomas's rallies said they agreed with him but that they were going to vote for Roosevelt simply to make sure Hoover would be thrown out. These people were acting upon what socialists would then have dismissed as "the theory of the lesser evil." Rail as they might against this pragmatic outlook, the socialists could do little to break it. In truth, it broke them.

By 1932 or 1933 the Socialist Party had reached a dangerous point—a bit like the Debsian party in 1912. It was no longer merely a sect but not yet a mass party. A sect can weather almost any political difficulties, often by simply ignoring them, or by tacitly counting on the likelihood that the world will simply ignore it. A mass party can maneuver and skirmish, its leadership aware that even when beset by severe internal disputes, all its segments have a stake in preserving unity. But a small socialist party can enjoy neither the sect's isolation nor the mass movement's protective brawn; it can command neither the sect's ideological discipline nor the readiness for compromise of a large party. Almost by definition, a small socialist party must be in trouble most of the time.

External pressures grew—pressures of reality—and soon these were refracted through the lens of internal factionalism. The question we must ask is: Could these pressures have somehow been withstood? Or at least checked and evaded?

At first glance the party's problems seemed mostly tactical; but in retrospect it seems clear that the socialists were being overwhelmed, like so many other people at the time, by the profound crisis of civilization that would beset our century. Consider the enormity of the problems: Was capitalism still a viable system or was it doomed to rapid destruction? Would the fascists sweep across Europe and perhaps America as well? Was Stalinism a mere aberration of the October Revolution or a new mode of social oppression? How should socialists analyze the "welfare state" in its rudimentary New Deal version, and what should be their political response?

Staring at these great blocks of difficulty, we should also remember that whatever understanding we have gained about them is partly a result of the confusions and grapplings of an earlier generation. What we know is what they had painfully to learn. And it was inevitable that among intelligent socialists there should be divergences of opinion. I shall not here rehearse the whole dreary story of the party's self-destruction through bitter factional disputes, but for what follows, I need briefly to sketch its major internal groupings.

On the right stood the Old Guard, hard and unyielding. As a youthful newcomer to the socialist movement, I was of course contemptuous of the Old Guard, and so was almost every other new member. How could I have known that I was aping the most conventional of conventional leftist attitudes? In the American left of those days anything not "revolutionary" was dismissed as beneath discussion; but that didn't bother the Old Guard, which gloried in its distance from the vulgar ferment of popular radicalism. Perhaps the Old Guard carried within itself too large a weight of historical pain—its admirers would say, historical knowledge. It had won the struggle against the communists in the garment unions during the 1920s, but that had drained much of its socialist spirit. It made of its very moderation a mannerism of excess. With a principled sort of grouchiness, it seemed almost intent upon showing that sectarianism can be found anywhere along the socialist spectrum. Some Old Guardists, like Morris Hillquit and Algernon Lee, were serious social democrats who looked upon Karl Kautsky as their mentor and the German party as their model. Others lived for the dry gratifications of anticommunism and, to be fair, the visible achievements of their unions.

I now think the Old Guard was more often "correct" in its political estimates than the leftists within the Socialist Party. It was more "correct" in its principled opposition to Stalinism and, after a time, certainly shrewder in its relation to the New Deal. But if its words were mostly right, its melody was mostly wrong.

In the chaotic atmosphere of the early thirties, the Old Guard socialists were unresponsive to whatever seemed new or unfamiliar. They had lost the taste for insurgency, something you might suppose socialists would have as their birthright. They failed to understand what it was about American life in 1933 that might drive a young person to the excesses of "leftism." Their minds still worked, but their imaginations had closed down. The socialist idea, no longer central to their lives, was like a weight of the past, hard to bear, hard to abandon. What had happened to the Old Guard is something that happens to many political and religious movements: its belief had not been quite destroyed, it had been *hollowed out.*

Opposing the Old Guard was a younger generation of radicals, mostly in New York, who called themselves the Militants. Their very name suggests they were really more concerned with activity than ideology. They wanted a "live" party, responsive to American needs and to the upheavals that were destroying bourgeois democracy in Europe. (It was the effort to combine these two responses that would bring them to grief, yet they were right to hope they could combine them.) Ideologically, the Militants tried to find some uneasy turf between reformist social democracy and doctrinaire Leninism. Inexperienced but ardent, they were not very good theoreticians, and their leaders, men like Robert Delson and Hal Siegel, would soon fade from the radical scene.

What troubled the Militants was any thought that, in the crisis of the thirties, socialists might succumb to notions about "patching up the system." And, even more, that after Hitler's victory, anyone should suppose reformism still a viable strategy for socialists. Partly, they wanted to impress Marxists to their left with the claim that they too were "revolutionary," though in fact they were neither temperamentally suited to Communist discipline nor prepared to accept its totalistic ideology.

How hard it is to imagine—I mean, *really* imagine—a historical moment other than one's own. Young socialists in 1934 or 1935 might not have heard of John Dos Passos's wisecrack that in the Depression era becoming a socialist was "like drinking near-beer." We might not have known that in 1932 a group of prominent writers moving leftward had called for "a temporary dictatorship of the class-conscious workers." But such ideas were in the air, and disconcerting to those of us still "mired" in mere democratic reformism. When we spoke at a socialist street rally, we would have to answer the needling question, "You really think the capitalists are going to give up without a fight?"—and the damnable thing was that not only the communists would ask this but also quite ordinary people, many of whom would soon be voting for Franklin Roosevelt. And the truth is, we weren't quite sure how to answer the question.

Somewhere in the middle of the party, and mostly from the middle of the country, was a loose assortment of younger people —intellectuals, trade unionists—not so ideologically rigid as the

Old Guard or the younger Militants. Perhaps the most promising, certainly the most open-minded segment of the party, these people wanted a movement at once active, flexible, and principled; and since they could not stomach the Old Guard, they went along with the Militants, though it would have been better if they had been a little more skeptical about the revolutionary phrasemaking of the latter.

I am suspicious of "generational" interpretations of politics, but I must confess that with regard to the Socialist Party in the thirties it is impossible to avoid at least some generational stress. The clash in style was striking. Not only did the Old Guard treat the ideas of the Militants as a repulsive sort of quasi-Bolshevism; it also found intolerable the enthusiasm of these naïve young comrades, their expectation that Norman Thomas booming out the credo of "socialism in our time" was something to be taken seriously. The youth had entered the movement in the hope of creating a new world, a new life, and now the old-timers came along, grumbling about defeats, mistakes, betrayals. Each generation spoke for its own portion of experience, and only if there had been in this country a line of socialist continuity, so that each generation would not have to start as if from the beginning, might this collision have been avoided.

Let me sketch, quite schematically, a few of the problems that overwhelmed the socialists of the thirties:

1. *The Soviet Union, the Communists, and the United Front*

Fifty years ago things looked different: theories of totalitarianism had scarcely been heard; the myth of Soviet progress still found credence; hardly anyone would have challenged the claim that the communists, for all their destructiveness, were an authentic part of the left.

Socialists were among the earlier principled critics of the Soviet regime. Though Morris Hillquit, in 1920, had gone so far as to propose that his party affiliate with the Third International, and Abe Cahan, editor of the *Jewish Daily Forward,* had written enthusiastically about Lenin's government, the Old Guard was by now, a decade or so later, shed of any illusions regarding Moscow. It opposed united fronts with the communists, distrusting their regimentation, their submission to Moscow, their deceitful tactics. By 1932 the Old Guard had achieved a considerable theoretical clarity about Stalinism, its leader Morris Hillquit writing that the Soviet system "presupposes a dictatorship that brooks no opposition . . . and is maintained by force and terror."[3] Not many people said this in 1932.

The left socialists tended, for a few years, to waffle. Some tried to draw a line between the economic base of Soviet society, which they applauded as an experiment in planning, and its political system, which they criticized for its lack of civil liberties. A few left-wing socialists, hungry for something to adore in those grim years, went further. Leo Krzycki, a not-very-brilliant trade unionist who succeeded Hillquit as Socialist Party chairman in 1933, praised Russia for having

> built herself up from a weak and poverty-stricken nation to a strong and prosperous one by concentrating on one principle—the elimination of private profit. . . . Because their electorate was uneducated and untrained in democratic methods, they had to exercise that control not only against the dispossessed aristocracy, but against those members of the working class who had not had enough vision to understand what they were doing. . . .[4]

Krzycki was not a fellow traveler, either openly or in disguise. But for Norman Thomas this was simply too much. He wrote in reply:

> The average man in the street or the factory is bound to think that [Krzycki's statement] is not merely a justification for dictatorship in Russia but of the extraordinary terror which unquestionably has been directed against Russian radicals. . . . We are on mighty dangerous ground when we give that impression.[5]

In a few years—certainly sooner than a great many American liberals—the left-wing socialists shook off their illusions about the Stalin regime. (Some, like their theoretician Haim Kantorovich, never had any.) They came to understand that with regard to a country where the state owns the entire economy, it is a mistake to speak as if economic base could be severed from political system. Years later, with characteristic grace, Norman Thomas admitted that "in 1932 [Hillquit] was nearer right in his judgment of what was happening in Russia than I was and certainly than the Militants were."[6]

More difficult was the problem of the united front. All through the late 1920s and the first few years of the 1930s, inspired by Stalin's inane discovery that "objectively, Social Democracy is the moderate wing of fascism," the communist movement had developed the bizarre theory of "social fascism" (which saw social democracy and fascism as "twins") and the equally bizarre tactic of appealing to socialist members for "a united front from below," that is, for unity against their own leaders. This tactic managed to chip away a few leftward-leaning socialists, but usually it merely antagonized the very people to whom it was addressed. The madness of the communist "Third Period" (1929–33)—and there are times when a politics can be accurately described only through the language of pathology—played a significant role in enabling Hitler to take power in Germany, since it foreclosed the possibility of linking social democrats and communists in united action against the Nazis.

The communist methods reached a savage climax in early 1934. Everyone on the left had been stirred—it was my initiation into the tragedy of Europe under fascism—by the resistance the Austrian socialists had put up against the attacks of the fascist Dollfuss government. The socialists organized a demonstration of solidarity in Madison Square Garden on February 16, but no sooner was the meeting opened than a communist contingent proceeded to disrupt through organized chanting and booing. Only one speaker, Frank Crosswaith, a black socialist, could make himself heard, and in a burst of rage he cried out that the communists were pigs "who will always remain pigs because it is in the nature of Communists to be pigs."[7] In pandemonium and disgrace, the meeting had to be adjourned.

The entire left responded with shock. The American Civil Liberties Union put the blame on the Communists for breaking up the meeting. A group of intellectuals, many of whom had supported the communist presidential candidate in 1932—John Dos Passos, Edmund Wilson, Meyer Schapiro, Lionel Trilling—sent the Communist Party an "open letter" of protest. The Old Guard felt vindicated, its paper denouncing the communists as "Ishmaels . . . moral lepers . . . unfit to associate with civilized human beings. . . ."[8]

Yet the clamor for a united front continued. In the atmosphere of the 1930s, *it had to*. During 1934 and 1935 the socialists were moving leftward and the communists, entering their Popular Front period, were moving rightward, so that for a little while they seemed rather close to each other.

There was a genuine urgency behind the clamor for a united front. Consider the feelings of the handful of socialists in Arkansas and Tennessee, who were trying, at the risk of their lives, to organize sharecroppers: didn't it make sense to work with anyone sharing their immediate objectives, no matter which idiotic theories Stalin advanced and his New York followers repeated? Or the socialists unionizing the automobile plants in Michigan: could they refuse out of hand to cooperate with communists who were also trying to organize the industry? You could say that they should collaborate as individual unionists while their parties went separate ways; but, if logical, this was not emotionally compelling. And many people feared a victory of fascism in the United States following its victories in Europe. Anytime we held a meeting during those years we would be peppered with questions about united fronts. What could we say? That the communists, if not by nature the "pigs" Frank Crosswaith had said they were, held to a politics that denied legitimacy to any other movement on the left and, indeed, required that all other movements be destroyed? We tried to say that, but in 1935 it was far more difficult to persuade people of this truth than fifty years later.

Let us visit a meeting of the Socialist Party's National Executive Committee in 1932 where a motion to meet with the communists to discuss united fronts was defeated by a vote of six to five. Here are comments made at this session, all of them, I think, with a certain cogency:

> Morris Hillquit:
>
> Such Communist proposals . . . are insincere and treacherous. [Their] invitation to form a "united front" bristles with gratuitous and deliberate slanders of our party. . . .
>
> Albert Sprague Coolidge:
>
> . . . Sooner or later a way will be found for common sense to triumph over this tragic and paralyzing split. . . . We should always be the last, rather than the first, to close the door. . . . The

> younger generations on both sides are showing tendencies to fraternize, disregarding the feud among their elders.
>
> Norman Thomas:
>
> I am skeptical whether the Communists will undertake united action on honorable terms. But for the sake of our . . . younger people, it must be made obvious that it is [the Communists] who sabotage the united front.[9]

Responsive to the sentiments of the younger socialists, Thomas understood that a blunt rejection of the united front would create dissatisfaction. He therefore tried carefully to clarify what he meant. A united front did not mean a fusion of the two parties, or a joint program, or suspending intellectual criticism. All it really meant was cooperation on specific issues—for instance, efforts to protect civil liberties.

Once the communists started, in 1934, to move toward a certain realism in appraising American politics, the idea of a united front grew more alluring. In 1936 there was a public debate between Norman Thomas and the communist leader Earl Browder, before twenty thousand people in Madison Square Garden, in which Browder was all bland amiability and Thomas more acerbic, once even provoking the large communist contingent by asking, "Is Russia so weak that it cannot afford, eighteen years after the revolution, to grant civil liberties to its citizens?" Yet the mere fact of such a debate signified a thaw in relations. And in 1936 there were some private talks between communist and socialist leaders about joint electoral campaigns, cooperation in the unions, and, it was even mooted, unification of the two parties. Nothing came of the first of these, a little of the second, and the third was a mere pipe dream. For there were too many deep divisions of principle. And there was the additional fact that the socialists, going left, were declining into a sect, while the communists, about to don the brilliant masquerade of the Popular Front, would soon be contemptuous of the scatter of Thomas's followers.

Might the socialists have coped with such problems? Only if they had had a strong, principled understanding of Stalinism, and been able to inculcate this among their members, could they have either withstood the appeals for a united front or entered into one without loss. But, like most other people, they were only starting to gain an understanding of Stalinism. Precisely the virtues of the socialists—their relative openness of mind, their democratic habits, their free-and-easy styles—made for weakness in coping with a better-disciplined rival. Thomas's thoughts about the united front were not at all bad; but he lacked a strong cohort of informed comrades who could cut a path between outright rejection and mindless acceptance. So the socialists lost among those who opposed and among those who favored the united front. Complexity of vision, intellectual doubt, humane tolerance are often a handicap in politics.

2. *Third Parties, Coalitions, and Splendid Isolation*

All through the 1930s there kept appearing local labor and farmer-labor parties, or third parties, expressing radical sentiments but refusing the Marxist options. In Wisconsin and Minnesota, these new parties were substantial, sometimes upsetting the traditional two-party system. Most socialists saw such developments as positive signs that the "old capitalist parties" were in trouble.

How, then, should socialists respond? Enter the third parties as an organized group in order to maintain a distinct identity? That was how things were done in England, where the Labour Party was a membership organization yet allowed other organizations to affiliate with it; but these local American parties rejected this kind of structure. Or should the socialists simply dissolve themselves into these new parties while hoping their individual members would help keep the idea alive? These were the main options, though a minority felt that socialists should keep strictly apart, on the ground that the options were still not truly socialist. Before examining these views any further, let me, however, turn back just a little to an earlier historical moment.

During the Debsian period, the socialists had accumulated some strength in the Northwest, attracting to their party a number of populists and agrarian radicals. In 1915 the North Dakota socialists helped organize the Nonpartisan League, which had a quite radical program, calling for the nationalization of railroads and grain elevators. Four years later, when the League captured the local Republican Party and won statewide office, its leaders introduced a number of reforms favorable to the farmers. But then, in part because of its success, the movement disintegrated. Similar movements arose in the states of Montana and Washington, merging with or taking over the local Democratic parties.

It was inevitable that socialists in the Northwest should be drawn to these strong yet ephemeral movements, and inevitable as well that once these movements peaked, the socialists should suffer. They lost a good part of their membership to the populist movements; they sincerely hoped the movements would succeed yet were skeptical of their ability to endure. Socialists are people who take the long view—in America they have to; and that alone separates them from most other Americans engaged in politics.

In 1924 the problem became acute. Robert La Follette, the progressive Senator from Wisconsin, headed a third-party national ticket, which the socialists endorsed warmly and the AFL supported nominally. Hoping this campaign would lay the basis for a new progressive or labor party, the socialists cast all their strength behind La Follette. The election result, from their point of view, was brilliant: La Follette polled almost five million votes, or 17 percent of the total, surely a large enough base for creating a new movement. But the unions, wanting quick victory, pulled out of the rickety organizational structure that had run the campaign, and soon, in consequence, the whole thing fell apart. Again, the socialists were the losers: their organization, neglected during the campaign, was smaller than before, and it took them several years to pull themselves together. One result was a certain sectarian hardening among both left and right socialists, a suspicion that getting involved in one of these quick-fix American crusades could only bring trouble.

By 1934 the problem grew still more acute. Farmer-labor parties were formed in Wisconsin, where the socialists were strong, and Minnesota, where they were weak. Local socialists entered these, sometimes in the hope of spreading their word, sometimes to escape the burdens of their own party. And again, when these local movements succeeded in becoming part of the political establishment or quietly declined into a mere memory, the socialists suffered losses. One difficulty was that socialists and nonsocialists who could work together on local problems came into conflict during presidential elections.

In 1934, Upton Sinclair, the novelist who had several times run as a socialist candidate in California, entered the Democratic primary for governor—and won. Around his EPIC (End Poverty in California) program, which came quite close to socialist "immediate demands," Sinclair built up a remarkable grassroots movement, which Jerry Voorhis, a socialist later to became a congressman, called "the nearest thing to a mass movement toward Socialism that I have heard of in America."[10] That it was a mass movement no one doubted; that it was "toward Socialism" Norman Thomas doubted.

The orthodox socialists were appalled—imagine going into one of the rotten old parties! Sinclair's own son, David, accused him of "insane opportunism," to which Sinclair mildly replied that he was just trying to "educate" the public. What Sinclair kept asking, and the socialists never found an adequate way of answering, was simply this: why was it worthy to push certain ideas outside the rim of the old-party structures and heresy to push the same ideas within it? One answer was that those ideas might be adulterated in the setting of old-party politics. So, indeed, they might; but if purity could be had only at the cost of impotence, was that not too high a price to pay? Another answer was that campaigns such as that of Sinclair would prove ephemeral, whereas the "basic task" was to build a lasting movement. Here the socialists had a point; but was it really impossible simultaneously to maintain an independent socialist voice while engaging in the kind of political foray Sinclair had undertaken? And as for lasting organization, it could be argued—as has Greg Mitchell, a student of the Sinclair campaign—that EPIC *did* have an enduring impact: "It helped tilt the New Deal to the left, it forever changed California politics, and it radicalized a generation."[11]

In any case, both the communists and what little remained of the socialists in California refused to support Sinclair, despite the enormous following he attracted. Victim of a campaign of slander, in which he was depicted as a threat to flag and family,

Sinclair lost the election, though he polled a very large vote. The socialist candidate did pitiably.*

The kinds of problem I've sketched here were all but insoluble as long as the socialists clung to a fundamentalist line that virtue consisted in voting only for a socialist or third-party candidate and sin was stamped forever on anyone who dared pull a lever for an old-party line. This article of faith was accepted by almost all socialists. I remember making speeches on the theme that "it's better to vote for what you want and not get it than to vote for what you don't want and get it." A nice slogan, and part of me still responds to it . . . faintly; but it didn't answer the situation in which, as happens in America, you might get a little more or a little less if you showed flexibility in the voting booth. Yet I feel a certain sympathy for the socialists who had to face these problems. Most Americans don't think in terms of enduring

---

*A word should be said about Huey Long, Father Coughlin, and the Technocrats. The first two had fascistlike characteristics; the last did not. But all, with their quick-fix schemes, threatened the socialists. Colorado party members were drawn to, in some cases captured by, Technocracy. Alan Brinkley, in his study of the Long and Coughlin movements *(Voices of Protest),* writes that "Long and Coughlin were winning the loyalties of the very people upon whom the future of the Socialist Party most depended."

H. L. Mitchell, socialist leader of the Southern Tenant Farmers Union, a precarious organization of sharecroppers which Thomas brought to national attention through his tours and speeches, wrote in 1935 about a Share the Wealth Club in Blytheville, Arkansas, led by men "who used to be Socialists." Another Southerner wrote Thomas that he had been with the party for thirty-five years and that "Huey Long is telling the people the things we have been telling them for a generation. They listen to him . . . while they thought we were fools."[12]

parties or ideologies; they see the political arena as a place in which to win immediate and limited results, after which there may again be some occasion for other forays, other coalitions. But the socialists *had* to think otherwise: this article of faith sustained them through years of waiting, at least until the faith collapsed, and then some of them would show a talent for opportunism that quickly brought them back to the ways of the homeland.

When it came to entering labor or farmer-labor parties, it was only tightly disciplined groups like the communists that could negotiate such a tactic while maintaining their organizational and ideological coherence. But the socialists, most of whom were sincere democrats, had neither taste for the covert nor talent for maneuver. They were the victims of their own rectitude, not the first or the last to discover that, in politics, virtue can sometimes undo the doer of good deeds.

3. *After Hitler's Triumph*

In 1933 it was not foolish to suppose that world capitalism had reached its final breakdown; it was only mistaken. Nor was it absurd to think we had entered a moment of historical apocalypse: we were wrong only as to its precise nature.

What most unnerved socialists, especially younger ones, was that this maniac-thug Hitler had destroyed every oppositional movement in Germany without meeting resistance from the social democrats, with their seven million votes, or the communists, with their five million. That the German left had gone down to defeat without offering even the last-ditch defense put up by the Austrian socialists a year later—this seemed not just a terrible humiliation but decisive proof of how hopeless was the reformist outlook at this point of world crisis. Any young socialist who kept even one eye on Europe found it hard to retain much faith in social-democratic gradualism. And we were right, I think, in keeping one eye on Europe, since that was where the fate of our century was being decided.

Here is a young socialist, Robert Alexander, writing in 1935 to Norman Thomas:

> The Austrian collapse is food for much thought. . . . When the most active Socialist Party in the world [is destroyed] in four days' fighting, something is wrong. . . . The Socialist idea is slow education and organization. That sounds well, but will the times wait for us to become organized, and let us convince the majority of the people? It does not look as if the American capitalists will shy away from Fascism any more than those of Europe did. . . .
>
> I believe that we should change our outlook to the extent of being willing to set up a forcible dictatorship here, if—when and if we are elected—the capitalists try to keep us out of power. . . .[13]

Here is the theologian Reinhold Niebuhr, some years later to become a liberal and dismiss his old socialist friends as mere "utopians," but in 1935 an ardent leftist scornful of Old Guard legalism:

> [The Old Guard] mouths the old platitudes about democracy. Its insistence that socialists must always remain within the bounds of legality is a perfect revelation of spiritual decay within socialism. No revolutionary group of whatever kind in history has ever made obedience to law an absolute obligation. . . .[14]

The Socialist Party was soon torn to pieces by factional strife, and since nothing can excite political people more than fratricide, the Old Guard rose up from its somnolence to combat "infantile leftism." But because the Militants won the sympathy of newcomers to the party, and because they worked out an alliance with Norman Thomas, they gained a majority. At the party's 1934 Detroit convention, the struggle came to a head over a Declaration of Principles put forward by the Militants. The party, they announced, would meet war with "massed war resistance"; would replace the "bogus democracy of capitalist parliamentarianism by a genuine workers democracy. . . ." And, in case the capitalist system collapsed "in a general chaos and confusion, which cannot permit of orderly procedure, the Socialist Party, whether or not it is a majority, will not shrink from the responsibility of organizing and maintaining a government under the workers' rule."[15]

This Declaration was adopted by about a two-to-one margin, thereby ensuring a split. It is worth quoting a few sentences from the debate, to give a sense of how people on the democratic left were thinking at the time:

> Devere Allen of Connecticut, a pacifist who wrote the final draft of the Declaration:
>
> If ever again a capitalist government of America masses into an imperialist war, to remain legal through that conflict would be to brand forever the Socialist movement with the mark of shame.
>
> George Kirkpatrick of California, a veteran from the Debsian era:
>
> You vote favorably [on the Declaration] and it will cause a grin and a loud laugh in many a Chamber of Commerce in this country. Many a ruffian sheriff will be delighted.

Powers Hapgood of Indiana, a crack union organizer and spokesman for the extreme left:

> The workers that I come in contact with say that their main objection to the Socialist Party is not that it is too radical, but that it is not radical enough.

Louis Waldman of New York, spokesman for the Old Guard:

> We are not Left enough! Dreamers! Visionaries! Romanticists! Why don't you adjourn and wake up tomorrow? We are not Left enough for American labor—that is the reason you want a suicidal Declaration today!

Norman Thomas:

> We say, in the event of the complete collapse of Government we will do thus and so. We say that if, after achieving power by constitutional means . . . there is a struggle against us, then we will act as brave men ought to act. Now what is there in that? What, but what Socialists have always said?[16]

Perhaps the most telling exchange came between Waldman and Joseph Coldwell, an old-timer from Rhode Island who had gone to prison with Debs for opposing World War I. Waldman, as if deliberately trying to provoke opponents, attacked the Declaration for being of doubtful legality. Whereupon Coldwell rose to say: "If the time has come when the Socialist Party members are afraid to say what they believe, the time has come to take down the red flag and the picture of Eugene V. Debs." To the delight of his young comrades, Coldwell ended with a grand flourish: "Goodbye, Comrades, if I don't see you again, I'll meet you in prison."[17]

There was something strangely misplaced about this debate. The Militants were not really revolutionists; few of them had any disposition for that Bolshevik discipline which was an unspoken premise of their Declaration; few understood what was prodding them to these phrases of bravado. What the Militants wanted was to register their dismay over the debacle of European social democracy; to rebel against the sluggishness of the Old Guard; to create a party of verve and energy. And their trouble was that they could find no way of doing this but to fall back on quasi-Leninist rhetoric. Both their thought and their language were inauthentic. For what could it possibly mean that a party of perhaps twenty thousand, a good many past their first flush of youth, threatened "mass war resistance"? What historical derangement could lead them to speak about "bogus democracy of capitalist parliamentarianism" at precisely the moment when the United States was starting one of its major exercises in social reform?

Norman Thomas, whose impulses were often better than his statements, tried to argue that the Declaration remained loyal to democratic values but also recognized that the threat of fascism could not always be fought through legal methods. But he knew, or should have known, that the best way to rally the American people against fascist demagogues was to invoke the values of the Declaration of Independence and the Constitution—to appeal, that is, to sacred standards, felt memories, powerful myths of a native democratic past. And this the Declaration of Principles made difficult.

The real issue within the socialist movement was about conviction, hope, energy—who still kept the faith. But people on the left often feel embarrassed when talking about such subjective matters; they must always look for ways to "deepen" the problem. Alas, they did.

4. The New Deal as Barrier

It is a commonplace of historical writing that American socialism in the 1930s was undone by Franklin Roosevelt's New Deal. Norman Thomas offers rueful confirmation of this view: "What cut the ground out pretty completely from under us was . . . Roosevelt in a word."[18] This summary yields a measure of truth, but, if examined closely, it turns out to be a bit too simple. Roosevelt's New Deal certainly bedeviled the socialists; it took from them a good part of their popular support; it advanced policies, especially between 1935 and 1937, that to an indifferent eye could seem "socialistic" and, even to a keen eye, overlapped with some of the socialists' "immediate demands." But to recognize all this is only a start in examining how the American socialists confronted the New Deal.

In the fall of 1933, several months after Roosevelt took office, Norman Thomas published a pamphlet in which he offered a preliminary and, in some respects, shrewd estimate of what Roosevelt was up to. Wrote Thomas:

> A nation which had persisted in a touching faith in laissez-faire economics [has] suddenly gone in for an immense degree of collective control through government. . . .
>
> [The purpose of the New Deal] is, with a minimum disturbance of the accepted economic order, to relieve the strain on it at the most dangerous points, to increase spending power for the masses, and to bring some sort of order in the capitalist chaos. . . .
>
> On the purely economic side we may conclude that, even on its own terms, to be successful over any length of time the New Deal must give us rapidly: (1) social control of money, banking and

credit; (2) general economic planning; (3) a more direct attack on the redistribution of income.[19]

A new, complicating note is struck in Thomas's 1934 book *The Choice Before Us:*

> To say that the Roosevelt Revolution, in so far as it was a revolution at all, was a revolution from laissez-faire to state capitalism, is not to deny the magnitude of some of its achievements. . . .
>
> The Roosevelt program makes concessions to workers in order to keep them quiet a while longer and so stabilize the power of private owners.[20]

In February 1936 Thomas made a radio speech with still another emphasis:

> Mr. Roosevelt did not carry out the Socialist platform, unless he carried it out on a stretcher. . . .
>
> Some of [what Roosevelt did] was good reformism, but there is nothing Socialist about trying to regulate or reform Wall Street.
>
> Not only is [the New Deal] not socialism, but in large degree this State capitalism, this use of bread and circuses to keep the people quiet is . . . a necessary development of a dying social order. . . .[21]

From such texts it is possible to extract a number of themes:

a) Necessary government intervention to shore up a crumbling capitalist regime;
b) Desirable social reforms to gain popular support and to quiet unrest;
c) Inadequacy of these reforms for coping with the misery of the Depression;

d) A long-range trend, stumbling and often not deliberate, toward "state capitalism."

Between 1933 and 1936 there was a shift in Thomas's analysis from flexibility to rigidity.* Each of his themes had some analytic cogency, but not equally so and not with equal political impact. There *was* a trend toward "state capitalism," if by that one means a greater degree of state control of economic life. But this was hardly the main immediate significance of the New Deal: not in 1933, when Roosevelt's improvisations stirred hopes in a dazed country, or in mid-1935, when the New Deal took a turn

---

*One of the reasons Thomas kept attacking the New Deal does him honor. He had become deeply involved with the Arkansas sharecroppers who, under the leadership of local socialists, had organized the Southern Tenant Farmers Union. These desperately poor people gained few, if any, benefits from Roosevelt's administration. The Agricultural Adjustment Act payments, which were made to farmers upon reduction of their acreage, displaced thousands of Southern sharecroppers, because landlords evicted them and held on to AAA payments for themselves.

Thomas kept needling Roosevelt and his Secretary of Agriculture, the liberal Henry Wallace, for their failure to help the sharecroppers —indeed, for averting their eyes when local authorities and planters' agents subjected the STFU to violence. James Green, in *Grass-Roots Socialism,* writes that Roosevelt "refused to risk losing the support of Senate leader Joe Robinson, a representative of the Arkansas planters, and so he agreed to the sacking of the pro-STFU people [liberals like Gardner Jackson and Jerome Frank] from the AAA. Henry Wallace went along with the 'purge,' too."[22]

Almost alone, Thomas kept the plight of the sharecroppers before the American public.

to the left, with important social legislation ranging from the Wagner Labor Relations Act to new and somewhat redistributive tax legislation. Besides, the Socialists might then have noted what did not dawn upon them until later: that some of the dangers they saw in the drift toward "state capitalism" might also well be present in a progress toward socialism.

Nor was it very persuasive in 1935 to point out the inadequacies of Roosevelt's social legislation, since to millions of Americans the startling fact was that the government was responding somewhat to their needs and easing somewhat their condition.

The trouble with the themes that Thomas proposed regarding the New Deal was that they did not fit into a coherent whole; there was no proper subordination of the lesser to the more urgent. But neither did most other analysts have a better grasp of the moment. The liberals weren't concerned with fundamental analysis—in America they seldom are. The conservative right saw Roosevelt as an enemy, while in fact he was the (somewhat oppressive) savior of the business class. And as for the left, it had become so accustomed during the 1920s to responding to the ideology of "rugged individualism" that it could not easily adjust itself to Roosevelt's improvisations. The Old Guard of the Socialist Party, delighted with the new strength of the garment unions, collapsed uncritically before the New Deal. The Militant Socialists adopted a posture of intransigent criticism, the rectitude of the pure. They rejected the New Deal as a mere tinkering with a broken-down system. No doubt, it was a kind of tinkering. But there ought to have been keener discriminations of analysis and attitude.

Some New Deal measures were ineffective. As late as 1941, there were still six million unemployed, and it was really not until the war that the army of the jobless finally disappeared. But

the social measures of the New Deal were of great consequence: Social Security, unemployment insurance, old-age pensions, the right to organize unions. The lasting contribution of the Roosevelt era was *the socialization of concern,* society seen as a community, not based as yet on egalitarian principles but at least modulating the heartlessness of "rugged individualism."

If in some respects the socialist criticism of the New Deal now seems too abstract—too chilly in relation to the hopes the New Deal set off among American workers, too aloof from the labor movement, which felt it had found a friend in Roosevelt—there is another respect in which the socialist response was not theoretical enough. The socialists lacked an adequate theory of the welfare state. They had come to think of capitalism as a fixed entity rather than a developing system with large capacities for adapting to new circumstances. And, by the same token, they thought of socialism as another fixed entity requiring a complete and probably abrupt historical transformation. Between these polar rigidities there was not much room for any theory of the welfare state.

By a welfare state I mean simply a capitalist society partly transformed and humanized through the pressures of internal, democratic insurgencies and also through improvisatory changes by a segment of the society's elite. The welfare state preserves essential traits of the capitalist economy in that the interplay of private or corporate owners in the market remains primary, but it also modifies the workings of that economy in that the powers of free disposal by property owners are politically regulated. Creating thereby a tension between government and economy, state and society, the welfare state acts to save capitalism from its own self-destructive excesses.

All the points Thomas made in his analyses of the New Deal could be fitted into such a theoretical approach. The inadequacies of New Deal reforms could be underscored; the dangers of interpenetration between state and corporations could be noted. What might then have eventuated was a subtle and balanced judgment such as the historian Richard Hofstadter would offer in 1948:

> The New Deal had accomplished a heart-warming relief of distress, it had achieved a certain measure of recovery, it had released great forces of mass protest and had revived American liberalism, it had left upon the statute books several measures of permanent value, it had established the principle that the entire community through the agency of the federal government has some responsibility for mass welfare, and it had impressed its values so deeply upon the national mind that the Republicans were compelled to endorse its major accomplishments in election platforms. But, as Roosevelt was aware, it had failed to realize his objectives of distributive justice and sound, stable prosperity.[23]

All this said, it could then follow that, in however qualified a way, the welfare state was, in leftist jargon, "progressive," and that it would consequently be a mistake to force a blunt counterposition between the left and the New Deal, even as it remained desirable to keep making serious criticisms.

What riddled the socialist ranks was not so much their analysis of the New Deal as the political position they deduced from that analysis. They took a stand of intransigent electoral opposition, insisting upon running socialist candidates in the 1936 election even though the bulk of the American working class and the unions favored Roosevelt. For socialists active in the unions this created an impossible situation: they had to choose between their unions and their party. In part because their livelihood depended on the unions, but more because they saw in the unions a growing dynamic force while their party was crumbling into a mere sect,

most of the socialists active in the unions felt obliged to leave the party. Many were unhappy about this choice; they wanted, somehow, to keep their socialist affiliation, if only as a matter of sentiment, while publicly supporting the political candidates endorsed by their unions.

One of these Socialists, and a left-wing Socialist at that, was Leo Krzycki, an official of the Amalgamated Clothing Workers Union who had been chosen national chairman of the party, a largely honorary post. When the executive board of the Amalgamated voted to endorse Roosevelt for president, he remained silent, asking to be "excused from voting." For the socialists this was an embarrassment, and Norman Thomas wrote Krzycki on May 18, 1936, "For you, our great labor spokesman, our Chairman . . . , without consulting any of us, silently to consent to the endorsement of Roosevelt—that was a blow." During the campaign Thomas discovered that he was often followed by Krzycki, speaking for Roosevelt. In Buffalo, according to Thomas's biographer W. A. Swanberg, Thomas encountered Krzycki, "an emotional man, [who] burst into tears as he explained . . . that he was forced to countercampaign. . . ."[24]

Some long-time socialists, like Emil Rieve, head of the Hosiery Workers Union, simply resigned from the party. Others, like Powers Hapgood and Franz Daniel, who had been on the far left within the party but were now important labor organizers, urged Thomas to "go easy" in his 1936 presidential campaign. For Thomas it must have been galling that these firebrands of yesterday should prove to be quite as susceptible to trade-union pressures as those who had criticized him from the right. In any case, the Socialist Party paid heavily for its intransigence, polling a mere 187,342 votes, a severe decline from 1932.

Some of the socialists drifting away to work in trade unions or government agencies felt little pain or regret; their youthful radicalism would sometimes become merely a topic for bouts of nostalgia or self-mockery. But to a good number of socialists the conflict between party and unions—almost a conflict between two realms of existence—brought considerable pain and regret.

Powers Hapgood had come into the party as a young man, quickly rising to leadership in Indiana, and by the early 1930s taking a place on the party's National Executive Committee. He then stood at the party's extreme left, adhering to a tiny, quasi-Leninist "Revolutionary Policy Committee." Hapgood came from a distinguished American family of writers and intellectuals; he had gone to Harvard; but his deepest inclinations were those of the labor activist. For a time this bright and lively man was involved with the Progressive Miners of America, a small independent union in Illinois engaged in bitter conflicts with John L. Lewis's United Mine Workers. Once the big industrial union-organizing drives began, Hapgood made his peace with Lewis and became a free-lance troubleshooter for many of the new unions, repeatedly involved in organizing campaigns. Lewis, as head of the CIO, never quite trusted him, but was shrewd enough to value his skills and devotion.

For a man like Hapgood, whose radicalism ran deep, the need—as he began to see it—to choose between party and unions was tragic. Refusing to follow those who dropped out of the party, he maintained formal membership but no longer took an active role. As late as 1940, though he hoped Roosevelt would defeat Willkie, he voted for Norman Thomas because, as he jokingly wrote to his parents, "I have one thing in common with Jim Farley, party loyalty. . . . I can't change my loyalty as quickly as others do."[25]

One day in the spring of 1939, Hapgood ran into an old

left-wing comrade, Franz Daniel, now organizing for the Amalgamated Clothing Workers. For anyone who, even from a distance, can share something of Hapgood's torn loyalties, there is a certain pathos in a description of this meeting he sent to his wife:

> When Franz Daniel learned I was here [in New York City] he came up to the hotel and we sat for five hours. . . . It seems foolish, but it wasn't, as we were talking about the problems we were all worried about—we are all working for CIO unions, but is our work helping Socialism or not? The other two [Daniel and Philip Van Gelder, an official in the shipbuilding workers union] have dropped out of the S.P. because they think it useless. . . . They feel sad, however, at the pure and simple policy of the unions for which they are working. We discussed it for five hours and feel that some of us in the union movement must confer more frequently. . . . It was the first talk of this kind any of us had for years.[26]

Clearly, if the Socialist Party could not find a way of keeping such men in its ranks, its future was bleak.

The problem of electoral strategy arose in an especially acute form in Michigan. By 1938 the Socialist Party was reduced to several thousand scattered members; one of the few places where it still retained some influence was in Detroit. A number of talented young socialists—the Reuther brothers, Emil Mazey, George Edwards, and others—held important posts in the recently formed United Automobile Workers Union. When the Michigan Democratic Party, within which labor was already playing a major role, chose liberal Governor Frank Murphy to run for reelection in 1938, the great majority of unions came to his support. Within the socialist local in Detroit there now arose an agonized discussion over political strategy. The fundamentalists insisted on an independent socialist campaign in opposition to Murphy, no matter what the cost might be in the labor movement, while the Socialists in the UAW, then embroiled in a bitter factional struggle that placed them precariously between communist and anticommunist groups, felt they had to make at least a *pro forma* endorsement of Murphy. The organizer of the Detroit party, a young man named Ben Fischer, kept struggling to hold his ranks together. Copies of the correspondence between Fischer and the party leaders in New York and Chicago have come down to us; it forms one of the most painful records I have ever read concerning the difficulties of adjusting principle to practice and the damage rigidity can do to even the most valid of principles.

Norman Thomas tried to intervene, writing Fischer that he was unhappy with one proposed solution—that Walter Reuther announce a "friendly resignation" from the party in order to enable him to endorse Murphy without embarrassing his socialist comrades. Such a resignation, noted Thomas,

> will not be understood as completely friendly. It will lessen our influence . . . and the only reason that you now seem to think it necessary is that he may have to support Murphy in some fashion. *Aren't you going to be in a serious position if we have to let go every good union man who . . . is obliged to support a non-Socialist candidate?* Of the two evils—that is, Walter's resignation or the Party's failure to nominate against Murphy—I think the latter less harmful. . . . [Emphasis added][27]

This sensible advice was not followed by the Detroit socialists. For a number of them, electoral opposition to all capitalist candidates had become a kind of religion, or at least ritual. Though Fischer knew such a course could lead only to a humiliatingly small vote and the loss of valuable members in the UAW, he finally acquiesced in the strange idea that the Socialist Party run a candidate for governor but not campaign for him. The result, of course, displeased everyone. The socialist candidate received less than .3 percent of the vote; Murphy lost to the Republicans; and many labor people were angered with the socialists. Walter and Victor Reuther left the party, the latter in a somewhat friendlier spirit than the former; other socialist figures in the UAW started to drift away; the last center of modest party strength was soon gone.

It seems probable that, in the climate of the late thirties, no strategic adaptations could have long prevented a disintegration of the socialist group in the UAW. But certainly the purism of the party's leadership helped speed the decline. In a year or two there would be almost nothing left, many of the Militant bravos having followed their more temperate comrades out of the party and into union or government posts. All that remained was Norman Thomas and a handful of supporters—Norman Thomas burdened, aging, defeated, unbreakable.

For many people, all this may be a matter of indifference, at most curiosity. For those who still care about American socialism, it is a sad story. Could it have been different?

Certainty is unavailable, but I rather doubt that it could have turned out very differently. There are times when a confluence of pressures comes down upon us with a force that neither strength of character nor clenching of will can finally resist. Precisely in its youthfulness and hope, the Socialist Party of the thirties turned out to be pathetically vulnerable. Neither quite revolutionary nor merely reformist, it lacked the defenses that being either might have given it. Neither wholly dogmatic nor fully open-minded, it could not take advantage of the possibilities that either stance might have yielded.

With the tactical problems I have discussed, the socialists might somehow have coped. But how to reconcile a leftism induced by sensitivity to European events with the need for relating to the greatest wave of social reform this country had seen for many decades—this the socialists did not know. There was of course a possible formula (hindsight makes tacticians of us all), and that was to say that the political urgencies of European socialism did not necessarily have an immediate bearing on the United States, or, in left-wing jargon, to raise again the question of "American exceptionalism." But to do that would have been to violate a deep Marxist persuasion—that of the unity of the world economy, the presumed "final" crisis of world capitalism.

The Socialists were facing new and really terrifying political-intellectual difficulties. With regard to an understanding of Stalinism they were far ahead of most liberals and many conservatives, yet they were still stumbling toward a coherent view of this new historical phenomenon. As for the New Deal, their failures of analysis and politics are less excusable. They might have looked back upon the earlier, fainter versions of the welfare state under Theodore Roosevelt and Woodrow Wilson, or to the richer experiences of the European social democrats in creating and responding to the welfare state. Ideological purism cost the socialists heavily.

Still, a certain sympathy is in order, a certain readiness to put ourselves back into their place half a century ago and recognize how hard it was to respond to the bewildering crossfire of problems that beset them. *It was all too much:* pressures from too many directions, envisaged solutions quickly coming into conflict with one another.

Thomas and his comrades indulged in a "leftist" rhetoric that brought them moral comfort but no political gain. They were the victims of a fundamentalist Debsian theology regarding the American electoral process. They drove their best people into a hopeless clash between political conviction and trade-union role. They failed to grasp the imaginative hold that the Rooseveltian reforms had taken on the American working class. Had they only bent a little more, they might not have broken.

The one strategy that might, just barely, have saved a portion of the socialist movement would have been to transform the party into an association speaking for the values of socialism, offering a fundamental critique of capitalism, and nevertheless allowing its supporters to participate in the surge of Rooseveltian reform. Complex and two-sided, this strategy presumes a degree of discipline hard, perhaps impossible to achieve in a movement that was inherently undisciplined. At the time, all of us on the party's "left" would have regarded such an approach as rank betrayal. Toward the late thirties Thomas and a few others started gingerly to advance such an idea, but it met with indignant rebuff among the remaining stalwarts.

Even if such a strategy had been adopted, it would have met with very grave difficulties. Some socialists active in the unions might have retained formal membership in such a transformed movement, but its power to hold their interest and gain their energies would probably have declined—for how could it compete with the high drama of creating the great industrial unions? For other young socialists, such an organization would have seemed tame, uninspiring, or in the language of a later time, a "copout." We had not joined to gain "immediate demands," even if we dutifully rehearsed our list of them. We had joined because our imaginations had been fired by the vision of a new world. How to reconcile that vision with day-to-day issues was for the socialists a seemingly insoluble problem. Perhaps it still is.

The long-run collapse of American socialism in the decades since 1933 has of course had deeper historical reasons than anything the party did or did not do. A whole generation was haunted and destroyed by the terrifying rise of Stalinism, which led to a perhaps fatal besmirching of the socialist idea. In part because of the problems thrown up by Stalinism, the socialist idea itself came to be in a state of deep crisis. You could no longer hold, if you had any intelligence, to the simplicities of the Debsian era. Everything now seemed problematic, and the socialist idea more a theory to be rethought than a banner to be hoisted.

In their few intense years the socialists of the thirties had lived through almost all of the political torments of the century, and it would be rank presumption to fault them for failures we still share. But it would be merely feckless not to learn from their mistakes.

The Brilliant Masquerade: A Note on "Browderism"

Is there nothing, then, to emulate in the history of American socialism? Nothing for a younger generation that, even while recognizing the extent of past failures, might want to reassert the ideals of yesterday's socialists?

Of course there is. Figures like Eugene Debs and Norman Thomas remain models of selflessness. So too do thousands of nameless rank-and-filers. There is a continuity of idealism in the socialist enterprise, which binds together people of different generations and experiences. Yet, if it's political strategies with which we're concerned, I suspect that most of what we need to learn from the movements of the past is how to avoid repeating their mistakes. And not to acknowledge the magnitude of those mistakes would be a form of disrespect.

The irony of it all, a bitter enough irony, is that the most promising approach of the American left, one that apparently came closest to recognizing native realities, derives from the very movement that has done the most to discredit and besmirch the whole idea of the left. About 1935 the American Communist Party, responding to instructions from Moscow, initiated its Popular Front policies. These policies were conceived in bad faith and executed with bad faith. Yet such is the cunning, or malice, of history that if ever we are to see a resurgent democratic left in America, it will have more to learn tactically from the Popular Front initiated by the Stalinists than from those political ancestors whose integrity we admire. The question then becomes, Can we separate what was authentic in the Popular Front approach from the gross deceit of those who developed it?

I don't propose here to write a full-scale account of the Popular Front in the late thirties. You can find what is, I believe, a still-valid description in the book Lewis Coser and I published in 1957, *The American Communist Party: A Critical History*; more recently, Harvey Klehr has added much substantiating detail in *The Heyday of American Communism.* Let me simply gather some essential facts so that we can quickly come to a discussion of their significance.

The Third Period of communist politics (so designated in Moscow), which began in the late 1920s and ended about 1933, constitutes one of the most bizarre episodes of modern political experience. At a time when Hitler was approaching power, the Comintern (Communist International) declared the main enemy of the working class to be . . . the Socialists. The Comintern Executive declared: "In countries where there are strong Social Democratic parties, fascism assumes the particular form of Social Fascism. . . ." From such premises the Communist International proceeded to an ultra-left strategy, one that in America meant proposing a "united front from below" with the socialist rank-and-file against the socialist leadership and, more important, trying to organize dual unions, that is, communist-controlled "revolutionary" unions in opposition to the established labor movement. The result was disaster for those scattered groups of workers that joined the dual unions, and isolation for the Communist Party (CP) itself. By about 1933 this policy had brought the American party to a point of exhaustion and impasse, so much so that during the greatest economic crisis American capitalism has ever suffered, the CP could not grow beyond a few thousand members. For about a year and a half it stumbled politically, clinging to some of the old ultra-revolutionary rhetoric even as it now proposed "united fronts" (from above, this time) to the socialists.

That the CP had driven itself into a blind alley with its Third Period madness has led some historians—those who would like retroactively to bless it with just a little authenticity—to argue that for reasons of its own the party was inching toward a Popular Front policy even before Moscow mandated it. There is precious little evidence for this claim, and it quite ignores the reality that for many decades the party functioned as a slavish dependent of Moscow. The initiative for the Popular Front came during the 1935 Seventh World Congress of the Comintern, notably in a speech by Georgi Dimitroff, the Bulgarian communist who had courageously defied Hitler during the Reichstag fire trial. The American CP did not, however, fully articulate the new Popular Front line until the spring of 1936, when its two main leaders, Earl Browder and William Z. Foster, visited Moscow. Harvey Klehr picks up the story:

> They arrived [in March] shortly after the signing of the Franco-Soviet Pact. . . . Browder remained reluctant to endorse Roosevelt [openly—I.H.], feeling that Communist support might give

> Roosevelt one million votes and cost him five million. The Comintern leadership digested this information for two weeks and then gave Browder the authority to decide how best to aid Roosevelt's reelection. In a private conversation Dimitroff told Browder that he alone could handle such a delicate and convoluted strategy: to run for President while trying to avoid harming the interests of another candidate.[1]

Browder immediately took to the new line, his only problem being over how best to execute it. Foster, traditionally more militant, had private hesitations, and somewhat later indulged in semipublic grumblings—a stance that reduced him to a mere figurehead in the party all through the Popular Front years.

Behind the new communist line was a perception in Moscow that the threat of Nazi Germany required the Soviet Union to find allies in the liberal bourgeois countries. The communist parties in those countries would have to make a sharp turn to the right, abandoning their revolutionary positions and declaring themselves warm allies of social democrats, liberals, and moderate bourgeois parties. In the United States this meant, formally or informally, to become part of the loose but strong alliance that Roosevelt had forged in behalf of the New Deal.

Yet to speak of the Popular Front in the vocabulary of revolutionary/reformist is, in very important ways, misleading. The Popular Front policy represented neither a conversion to liberal politics and values, since for one thing it coincided with the peak of the Russian terror, nor a lapse into social-democratic reformism, since at every crucial point the loyalty of the communist parties remained not with their own liberal bourgeois states but with the Russian state-party. Because the Stalinist movement, like the Stalinist state, represented something novel in history, its policies could be analyzed much more profitably through categories like "totalitarian" than the traditional Marxist ones.

The communist parties now pushed their new line to extremes far beyond the formulas of the Seventh World Congress. An impulse to drive its ideas to an ultimate limit—indeed, close to the point of parody—seems inherent in totalitarian movements, but in the thirties there were also substantial reasons of expediency for doing so. If what mattered most was finding strong allies for the Soviet Union, then there was no necessary reason for confining the search to liberal parties. In countries where liberals were weak, the communists began to look further to the right. They came to see that a certain kind of conservative, intuitively sympathetic to the authoritarian state wherever it might be, could prove a better ally—one less inclined to ask embarrassing questions about concentration camps—than many liberals. In the United States, where liberalism was ascendant during the thirties, the communists did not have to look much beyond them, though during World War II the CP would advance a policy of the "Democratic Front" that included major segments of capitalism.

Starting about 1935, then, the American communists began one of those extraordinary self-transformations—or perhaps a still more extraordinary shuffling of public masks—that are an integral part of communist history. The "vanguard party," which had declared the New Deal a precursor of fascism, now became an enthusiastic and uncritical supporter of Roosevelt. Marxist jargon was replaced by the slogans of liberalism and an appropriation—sometimes skillful, often absurd—of Jeffersonian rhetoric. Communism was declared to be "twentieth-century Americanism" and Browder "the new John Brown of Ossawatomie." The CP presented itself as just another American party, prepared to collaborate with everyone desiring peace, justice, and a joint front against fascism. The party as an institution gave itself a remarkable paint job, changing from bright red to a lively red, white, and blue. Everything was changed—the language of the party press, the appearance of party offices, the conduct of local party branches—all with the purpose of inserting the CP into the mainstream of American politics. The leadership was brushed and brightened too. Old functionaries were banished to minor posts, and new, more attractive leaders, like Benjamin Davis of Harlem and Eugene Dennis of the Northwest, became Browder's close collaborators. A group of communist and communist-influenced trade-union leaders became prominent—Julius Emspak, Harry Bridges, Joseph Curran, Michael Quill—who lent substance to the party's enterprises. And in the intellectual world, the Popular Front policy, though challenged with some success by the small anti-Stalinist left of *Partisan Review,* brought enormous influence to the party and its linked agencies.

Politically, the Popular Front meant, above all, to penetrate the institutions and organizations of the New Deal—to a minor extent, the governmental apparatus, and to a larger extent, the Democratic Party and allied local political groups, like the Commonwealth Federation in the state of Washington, the Farmer-Labor Party in Minnesota, and the American Labor Party in New York. Nowhere did the Communist Party—Popular Front or not—become the dominant political force that later professional anticommunist writers would say it was; but in these and other states it became a *significant* force, one that politicians in the Democratic Party had to reckon with, either openly or through intermediaries. The strength of the CP was now to be measured less in its own membership, though by 1939 it had somewhere between seventy and eighty thousand members, than in the influence that a network of front groups and quasi-independent allies gave it. By now the party cared more about steering the politics of the liberal "mass movement" in which it participated than in scoring direct organizational gains. And in the course of this expanded influence, many CP people developed notable political skills or put to effective use skills they brought from their past. Some even learned important lessons about American political life. Communists in the state of Washington, writes Harvey Klehr, "discovered just how open and permeable American political parties were. *'You are a member of whatever you say you are,'* Terry Pettus [a local CP figure] recalled, explaining how a relatively small group of activists could win control of a large segment of the Democratic Party."[2] Pettus's "discovery"—minus, of course, the Stalinist habit of manipulation—might have profited the socialists of both the Debsian and Norman Thomas eras.

The communists were able to gain thousands of new recruits, as well as still more sympathizers, during the Popular Front years because they managed to combine an extraordinary range of political and emotional appeals. There was the Soviet Union, seen by some as the bulwark of a new socialist society and, for those with more authoritarian tastes, as the base of Stalin's dictatorship. There was the popular blend of New Deal outlooks and CIO militancy. There was the stirring cause of Loyalist Spain, under assault by General Franco's fascists. All of these political themes were linked with the hoop of antifascism, effective enough until the day in 1939 when Hitler and Stalin signed their pact and the Popular Front met sudden death. You could think of yourself as a revolutionary, you could think of yourself as a militant unionist, you could think of yourself as a "progressive," you could even think of yourself as a liberal of sorts, and still lend support to the communist movement or at least its many-colored front organizations.

Nowhere was the success of the CP more striking than in the newly formed CIO unions. The party's turn toward the Popular

Front coincided roughly with the great wave of strikes and union organizing, but it's interesting to note that Browder and his associates were at first rather cautious about the CIO—indeed, a shade reluctant to get involved. For this, I'd speculate, there were two reasons: the CP had been thoroughly burned during its dual-union adventures of the late 1920s and now looked uneasily at anything that might open it to the charge of returning to that disastrous policy, and the Popular Front as political outlook tended more to "class peace" than the upsurge of worker militancy that marked the early days of the CIO. As late as December 1936, because of his eagerness to stretch the Popular Front idea to include even the "labor lieutenants of capitalism" heading the AFL, Browder was still talking about the "unity" of the labor movement—even though the unions following John L. Lewis had left the AFL, and the organizing drive of the new CIO was virtually irresistible. It took a few months more for CP-controlled unions to bolt the AFL and affiliate with the CIO.

Lewis himself seems to have been a little surprised at the enormous response the new industrial unions were getting in the factories. He didn't, in any case, have enough organizers to take care of the locals that were springing up across the country. He had veteran aides from the United Mine Workers, but their number was limited and they lacked the rhetoric, the ideas, the idealism needed for organizing auto, steel, and other major industries. With more than a touch of cynicism, Lewis turned to the very communists he had fought so bitterly during the 1920s. And in early 1937 the CP was ready and eager. It had young people who were experienced, articulate, tough, and self-sacrificing. They knew how to write leaflets, paint signs, set up picket lines, and sometimes how to talk to American workers.

In late 1936 Lewis met with Clarence Hathaway, a top CP

figure, and in early 1937 Browder met with John Brophy, the left-leaning veteran unionist who in the past had fought hard against Lewis but now was serving as the CIO organizational director. A tacit deal was struck. Important figures in or close to the CP gained key posts in the CIO national office, most notably the shrewd Lee Pressman, who became the CIO's chief counsel and an influential adviser to Lewis. Dozens of communists were taken on as staff, especially in the Steel Workers Organizing Committee, which at one point, according to William Z. Foster, had sixty communists among its two hundred full-time organizers.

The CP was now gaining a chunk of real power—control of major unions (electrical, metalworkers, West Coast longshore, New York transport, etc.) and a strong foothold in the auto workers' union. But just to plant organizers loyal to the CP wouldn't have been enough. Thousands of rank-and-file communists formed nuclei in the newly created unions, their skills and experience providing them with an enormous advantage over political adversaries and new members. And, to be fair, the CP unionists sometimes earned their trust. If there was tiresome work to do, they were ready. If leaflets had to be distributed on a cold winter morning before an Akron rubber plant or a New York subway station, party volunteers were on hand. The communists were indefatigable meeting-goers, often caucusing before meetings, ready to sit out intraunion opponents into the early hours of the morning, and working with a persuasive mixture of moral fervor and cordiality toward almost everyone to their right.

In important respects the Popular Front line fitted perfectly the temper of the time in which the major CIO drives took place. Popular Frontism during the late 1930s permitted the communists to be combative enough to participate actively in the CIO drives, yet moderate enough to accept the CIO's dominant New Deal or liberal sentiment. As long as the CP could maintain this balance it was able to satisfy some of the more aggressive elements in the unions while staying on good terms with most of their leaders.

Much of the credit for the success of the Popular Front policy must go to Earl Browder, by now uncontested boss of the party and increasingly its public spokesman. People like me, veterans of the small phalanx of "premature" anti-Stalinism, were inclined to underestimate Browder, seeing him merely as what in fact he was, a docile Stalinist functionary, mediocre in style and appearance, a drab speaker, a pedestrian writer, and a "theoretician" whose few ventures into Marxist casuistry fell painfully flat. But we missed an essential point: that for the Popular Front Browder was the right man, some intuitive elements of his shrewdness and caution now coming into play. He had a sharp eye for the neat maneuver, the clever arrangement; he knew how to flatter and work with trade-union allies; and he seemed like an eminently respectable fellow, indeed, somewhat like a small-town lawyer or politician. As became clear in later years—this would lead to his expulsion from the party in early 1946—Browder not merely accepted the Popular Front line; he warmed to it, he enjoyed it, and he came, with evident sincerity, to believe in it. The moment had found its man—perhaps a small man, to be sure, but just right for the job.

To skeptics it might seem that the Popular Front venture carried within itself an element of excess, even parody. When Robert Minor, an old CP hack, wrote lyrically about Earl Browder's Americanism, invoking the memory of ancestor "Littleberry Browder [who] was sworn in as a soldier of the Continental Army of General George Washington," some of the party veterans must have chuckled (quietly). When the Daughters of the American Revolution forgot in the spring of 1937 to celebrate Paul Revere's ride and the Young Communist League paraded along Broadway with a sign, "The DAR Forgets but the YCL Remembers," some sense of the absurdity of it all must have struck the more intelligent communists. Or when the Young Communist League at the University of Wisconsin explained that its members were no different from other American youth ("We go to shows, parties, dances, and all that") except that its members "believe in dialectical materialism as a solution to all problems," even the truest of true believers must have been amused at this confusion of Third Period and Popular Front language. But did it really matter? Excess, hoopla, blarney are all so deeply ingrained in American politics, the communists could add their distinctive touch without disturbing many people. And if there sometimes was a strain of conscious self-parody in the Popular Front line, that too might well have been a token of loyalty in carrying out the will of the collective, the wisdom of the party.[3]

The single greatest irony of the Popular Front lies in the thought that the American communists might never have managed it successfully but for the sectarian "training" of their Third Period. It was during the Third Period, with all of its inanities about "social fascism" and all its disasters of dual unionism, that the CP developed a steeled inner cadre of a few thousand people. These were men and women who, either as full-time functionaries or part-time volunteers, gave "the whole of their lives" to the movement. Anyone, it might be said, who could remain faithful to Stalinism both in and after the Third Period *had* to be a true believer. These people had become accustomed to seeing the ideal of communism as totally inseparable from support for whatever policies came down from Moscow. They followed the party line through every wrenching turn, not simply because they had been broken to obedience (though some had), but because they really believed that each strategic maneuver of the Comintern furthered the ultimate goal to which they were pledged. At once idealistic and cynical, selfless and corrupted, they responded to the Popular Front with the same blinding credence that they had shown to the ultra-revolutionary policies of six or seven years earlier. And, often enough, with more enthusiasm.

As the CP gained thousands of new members during the Popular Front years—very few of them "revolutionary" in either Old Bolshevik or Stalinist styles—it began itself, internally, somewhat to resemble a Popular Front. Some of its old-timers still regarded themselves as revolutionary Leninist-Stalinists waiting for the happy moment when the party returned to open statements of fundamental doctrine. Often these old-timers were industrial workers who had accepted communism as an integral faith and could not be budged from it by appeals to tactical shrewdness. (A former CP leader has remarked privately that some of these veteran comrades saw the Popular Front policy as a device for "the goyim," the uninitiated, while they, the veterans, wordlessly clung to the revolutionary formulas of the past.) Others sincerely believed the party's new slogan that "Communism Is Twentieth-Century Americanism." And still others, perhaps a good many of the activists, suppressed a bit of doubt concerning the relation between old dogmas and new methods.

The party now accepted with equanimity the fact that many of its new members were inactive and some merely paid their dues once or twice a year. No longer did it make exorbitant demands on the time, energy, and money of its members, such as had been the custom in, say, 1929 or 1931. The party did not expect—and, given the elaborate political maneuver that the Popular Front represented, it did not even desire—that each member be able to articulate the finer points of doctrine or know about the complex shifts of party line that had preceded the Popular Front. On the face of it and—to a degree hard to determine—in reality as well, the American Communist Party became a party like other parties.

But not really, not finally. Within the new, loose-structured Communist Party of some seventy to eighty thousand members there remained an old skeletal "vanguard" of perhaps three or four thousand. The basic policy directives still came from Moscow, although party headquarters in New York was now quite flexible in the ways it imposed its dictate on local units or comrades active in trade unions. The very nature of the Popular Front required a certain improvisation of tactics and looseness of approach, and it was part of Browder's skill to recognize this. Where the party remained inflexible was in defense of the Soviet Union, which meant in defense of the Stalinist terror of the 1930s, the forced collectivization, which had brought death to millions of Russian peasants, and the Moscow Trials, which cut down a good part of the Old Bolshevik leadership. Not a shrewdly worked-out response to American circumstances during Roosevelt's presidency, but obedience to the needs of the Russian state-party, lay at the heart of the party's actions. When, however, American circumstances and Russian needs coincided or overlapped, the party thrived.

So it's with only a touch of exaggeration that we can say that together with the new Browderite flabbiness there remained, in the shadows, the old Fosterite toughness. (With a touch of exaggeration because Foster was now accepting, somewhat grudgingly, the Popular Front line, and Browder had never shown any resistance to the ultra-leftism of the Third Period.) The Stalinist cadre still ran the party. A few of the old leaders were privately troubled by Browder's "reformist" caprices; a few were biding their time in the hope of seeing a change of party regime and political line. But in many others, especially those who had become involved in "mass work" and the trade unions, there was a growing inclination to take the Popular Front at face value, especially once their new circumstances as leaders of growing segments of the party and increasingly powerful unions became more and more attractive.

Let us not forget a simple fact that some historians of American communism do tend to forget: communists, even hardened communist leaders, remain human beings—often enough fanatical, often enough with moral sensibilities coarsened, but, still, human beings susceptible to the desires and needs that most of us experience. A second-level party leader who had been section organizer, say, in Cleveland during the early thirties and had led demonstrations that brought him stitches in his head and months in jail, might now find it exceedingly pleasant to be leading a party that had opened an attractive headquarters, enjoyed good relations with local politicians and trade-union leaders, and could attract seven or eight thousand people to a rally when Earl Browder came to Cleveland. A section organizer in Harlem, where the party had counted a mere straggle of comrades during the early thirties, might now find it decidedly pleasant to be able to reach Adam Clayton Powell on the phone whenever he chose, to enroll hundreds of new black members, and to lure a brilliant array of Harlem talent when the party ran a big social event. An old, battered activist could now feel a sense of growing authority in heading, say, a large Massachusetts local of the electrical workers' union, or a local of the California maritime workers' union, sheltered within the CIO and favored, more or less, by John L. Lewis. As for the top union leaders who belonged or were close to the CP—men like Julius Emspak, Joseph Curran, Harry Bridges, and Mike Quill—they were starting to enjoy a taste of real power. They were negotiating contracts that covered thousands of members; were disposing of significant sums of money (some of it drained off to the party and its front groups); were dealing and wheeling with other union leaders and political figures who wanted their support. Respectability, comfort, secretaries, good salaries, docile staffs, admiring followers—all came together to soften and allure.

Let us put aside both the communists for whom the Popular Front was a necessary digression from the path of revolution and the recently acquired members, political naïfs, to whom it was an attractive substitute for that path. The most interesting group of party members consisted of people with some standing and experience who, almost against their will and perhaps to their own surprise, came to value the Popular Front as both a shrewd maneuver and more than that—indeed, may even have come to believe that, for America at least, this was the way radicals should go. How many such people there were, no one knows, but that they numbered in the thousands seems a reasonable speculation. We may doubt that many of them went so far as to recognize that the Popular Front really signified a break from classical Leninism and even, perhaps, the start of an adaptation to the special circumstances of American life. But most changes of thought occur hesitantly, and language always lags behind impulse and feeling. The CP trade-union leaders were especially important in this respect, since they valued, understandably enough, the achievements and power of their unions and preferred that the CP follow a line that would not force them to an irrevocable choice between party and union. Short of that, the communist trade-union leaders could help the party in dozens of ways, while the party could help them by providing reliable followers who would shore up their positions within the unions. It was a comfortable relationship. Most top union leaders never attended a local party meeting, because of caution or lack of time, and would instead keep in touch with either Browder himself or one of his aides. The old firebrands and seasoned organizers who held posts of secondary leadership within communist-dominated unions sometimes allowed themselves an open connection with the party, or simply called themselves "progressives," a euphemism that everyone in the unions understood. Thereby these party veterans could preserve their sense of political virtue while in day-to-day union business gradually assuming some of the traits of conventional union leaders.

The more important communist or communist-inclined union leaders seldom tolerated party interference on strictly union matters, and under Browder's shrewd prompting, the party bureaucracy learned to accept this state of affairs as it might not have during the early thirties. For the party knew it wasn't really in a position to dictate trade-union policy to powerful figures like Mike Quill of the Transport Workers Union or Joe Curran of the National Maritime Union. The party remained content with a division of influence, power, and function: it not only gave such union leaders a free hand, it also supported them consistently within their unions, and in turn they almost always made the kinds of political statements that were wanted.

All the while, within the party there remained a hard core, an increasing number of them now serving as paid functionaries in the bewildering array of organizations the party controlled.

There had been some changes in the hard core, a moderate "circulation of the elites," but its authority was unchallenged and its obedience to the handful of party leaders who formed the Politburo unqualified.

Because it remained firm at the center, the party could afford, in applying the Popular Front, to be loose at its edges. Because the hard core lived by an inner motive and esoteric doctrine, it could maintain an impressive level of discipline in adjusting to the gymnastics of the Popular Front. Had the CP really become a social-democratic party, or any other sort of democratic party, it would probably have had to suffer the inner contentiousness, the factionalism, and the incoherence that must sooner or later beset all such parties. But the combination of inner allegiance and doctrine with public masquerade proved to be remarkably successful, transforming the party from a wretched little sect to something like a mass movement, not yet a major force in the country but able to exert notable influence in many social institutions and arenas of culture.

The question then remains, and we cannot be at all sure of the answer: Suppose a policy somewhat like that of the Popular Front (call it "coalition politics") were pursued by an American left-wing movement in good faith and without Stalinist absurdities, and suppose, further, that it were pursued out of an honest wish to advance the socialist idea by inching forward with the social reforms we associate with the welfare state. Let us leave aside the public difficulties of such a politics and focus only on the problems it might create within a socialist movement. How far could such a movement go without abandoning, in all but name, its fundamental principles? Would its increasing absorption with "small" immediate issues reduce it to a mere agency or accomplice of the *status quo*? Might not its most active people lose themselves in their day-to-day tasks, gradually forgetting the deeper purposes of the movement? And how long could it avoid inner divisions and perhaps open splits regarding the problems certain to follow from its engagement with "real" politics?

We cannot say. We can only acknowledge somewhat ruefully that even the example of the Popular Front is an ambiguous one. Democratic radicals can learn a good deal from it, both what to avoid and what to emulate—avoid the deceits of Stalinist manipulation, emulate the effort to engage with the social and political problems that occupy American society. But always there is the caution that what succeeded as a brilliant masquerade might look rather different if undertaken out of democratic good will.

Why Has Socialism Failed in America?

America never stood still for Marx and Engels. They did not attempt a systematic analysis of the possibilities for socialism in the New World, but if you look into their *Letters to Americans* you will find many interesting *aperçus,* especially from Engels. Almost all the numerous theories later developed about the fate of American socialism are anticipated in these letters.

As early as 1851, when the socialist Joseph Weydemeyer migrated to the United States, Engels wrote him:

> Your greatest handicap will be that the useful Germans who are worth anything are easily Americanized and abandon all hope of returning home; and then there are the special American conditions: the ease with which the surplus population is drained off to the farms, the necessarily rapid and rapidly growing prosperity of the country, which makes bourgeois conditions look like a beau ideal to them. . . .[1]

It isn't far-fetched to see here a germ of what would later be called "American exceptionalism," the idea that historical conditions in the United States differ crucially from those set down in the Marxist model for the development of capitalism, or differ crucially from the way capitalism actually developed in Europe. Consider those remarks of Engels: a recognition of, perhaps irritation with, the sheer attractiveness of America; a casual anticipation of the Turner thesis in the claim that "surplus population is drained off to the farms"; a wry observation about American eagerness to accept the bourgeois style, though this might better have been phrased in the language of American individualism.

At about the same time, Marx was taking a somewhat different approach. "Bourgeois society in the United States," he was writing, "has not yet developed far enough to make the class struggle obvious"[2]; but he also expected that American industry would grow at so enormous a rate that the United States would be transformed into a major force in the world market, delivering heavy blows against English imperial domination.

Now, if one cares to, it is possible to reconcile Engels' approach with that of Marx. Engels was thinking tactically, about the problems of building a movement, while Marx was thinking historically, about events anticipated but not yet encountered. Marx was asking why the social consequences of the rise of capitalism, such as an intensified class struggle, had not yet appeared in the United States—even though, according to his theory, these consequences were inevitable. He was "testing" a particular historical sequence against his theoretical scheme, and this led him to believe that capitalism would emerge in the United States in its purest and strongest form—purest, because unencumbered by the debris of the precapitalist past, and strongest, because able, both technologically and financially, to leap past the older capitalism of England. Thereby, he concluded, the United States would—or was it, should?—become "the world of the worker, par excellence,"[3] so that socialist victory might even occur first in the New World. Here Marx was verging on a materialist or "economist" reductionism, and he would repeat this line of reasoning some thirty years later, in 1881, when he wrote that, capitalism in the United States having developed "*more rapidly* and *more shamelessly* than in any other country,"[4] the upsurge of its working class could be expected to be all the more spectacular.

Engels's observations, because more "local," tend to be more useful. He writes in his 1891 preface to Marx's *The Civil War in France*: "There is no country in which 'politicians' form a more powerful and distinct section of the nation than in North America. There each of the two great parties which alternately succeed each other in power is itself controlled by people who make a business of politics. . . ."[5]

Had the later American Marxists picked up Engels's tip here, they might have avoided some of their cruder interpretations of the role of the state in this country. More interesting still is Engels's introduction to the 1887 reprint of his book *The Condition of the Working Class in England,* where he acknowledges "the peculiar difficulties for a steady development of a workers party"[6] in the United States. Engels first makes a bow toward the overarching Marxist model: ". . . there cannot be any doubt that the *ultimate* platform of the American working class must and will be *essentially* the same as that now adopted by the whole militant working class of Europe. . . . [Emphasis added]" Engels would elsewhere stress the "exceptionalist" aspect, largely tactical, of the American problem. In order to play a role in politics, he says, the American socialists "will have to doff every remnant of foreign garb. They will have to become out and out American. They cannot expect the Americans to come to them; they, the minority and the [German] immigrants [in the Socialist Labor Party] must go to the Americans. . . . And to do that, they must above all else learn English."[7]

What may we conclude from all this? That, like other thinkers, Marx and Engels cherished their basic models; that the more closely they examined a particular situation, the more they had to acknowledge "deviations" from their models; that they anticipated, quite intelligently, a good many of the major themes in the discussions about socialist failure in the United States; and that in their efforts to suggest adaptations of the nascent socialist movement, mostly immigrant in composition, to the American setting, they were not very successful. You might suppose, however, that Engels's proposal that the Germans learn English would be regarded, in leftist terminology, as "a minimum demand."

If I have overstressed the differences in approach between Marx and Engels, it is for a reason: to show that both the orthodox view of later socialists, clinging to the authority of the Marxist model, and the heterodox emphasis upon American distinctiveness, can legitimately be attributed to the founding fathers of Marxism. An interesting comment on this comes from Theodore Draper in a personal communication: "Whenever the two old boys considered real conditions in real countries, they gave way to the temptation of 'exceptionalism' (I seem to remember that it crops up in their writings on India, Italy, Ireland as well). Reality always breaks in as 'exceptions' to the rule.*

---

*One notable exception, at the opposite extreme from the American, is worth glancing at. Among the Russian radicals of the second half

Werner Sombart's *Why Is There No Socialism in the United States?* first appeared in 1906, and though its thesis has been rendered more sophisticated in numerous later writings, it remains a basic text. I propose here somewhat to minimize—though not to dismiss—Sombart's reasons, which tend mainly

---

of the nineteenth century there was an intense and significant debate as to the possibility that socialist development in Russia might bypass capitalist and urban industrialization. Must Russia follow the familiar lines of Western development, or can it proceed along its own, "exceptional" path? The concrete issue was the *mir,* or traditional peasant commune. When the Russian Marxist Vera Zasulich wrote Marx in 1881 for his opinion, he devoted himself to this problem with much greater energy than to American problems—it may have seemed more important, or at least closer. After preparing four drafts of a reply, Marx sent the last one to his correspondent, writing that the account in *Capital* of the development of capitalism was "*expressly* limited to the *countries of western Europe*" and therefore provided "no reasons for or against the vitality of the rural community." He added, however, that he had become convinced that "this community is the mainspring of Russia's social regeneration."[8] Later he and Engels wrote that the *mir* could pass on to a higher form of "communal ownership" and avoid the "dissolution which makes up the historical development of the west . . . if the Russian Revolution is the signal of proletarian revolution in the West, so that both complete each other. . . ."[9]

Whether this judgment was correct need hardly concern us here. What matters is Marx's evident readiness to grant that Russia might be an "exception" to the developmental scheme of *Capital.* There is no similar readiness in his writings with regard to the United States, not even to the limited extent one finds it in Engels's letters; and one wonders why. An obvious reason is that Engels lived longer and, as

to stress objective historical factors standing in the way of socialism in America. But since he saw that some of these factors, like the supply of free land in nineteenth-century America, would not be operative much longer, he concluded—like the Marxists, though not one himself—that in a few decades socialism would thrive in America. In this prediction he was mistaken, and it is important to know why. Here, in schematic form, are some of the Sombartian "objective" factors that account for the failure, or at least difficulties, of American socialism:

1. Since this country had no feudal past, Americans could feel that as free citizens of a "new nation" they were able to express their needs and complaints within the democratic system; in consequence, the sense of class distinctions was much less acute here than in Europe.
2. Material prosperity in the United States, the result of a tremendous economic expansion, undercut the possibilities of socialist growth, since it enabled segments of the working class to gain a measure of satisfaction and imbued others with the hope that America would be their "golden land."

---

the gray eminence of the movement, had to cope with the hopeless sectarianism of the German exiles who formed the Socialist Labor Party in America during the 1880s. More speculatively, I would say that it was easier for Marx to grant an "exception" to a precapitalist economy mired in absolutism than to an economy becoming quintessentially capitalist, and easier, as well, to acknowledge the political consequences of a "basic" socioeconomic institution like the *mir* in Russia than the political significance of a "superstructural" element like the national culture of America.

3. The greater opportunities America offered for upward social mobility led most Americans to think in terms of individual improvement rather than collective action—they hoped to rise out of rather than with their class.

4. The open frontier, with its possibility of free or cheap land, served as a safety valve for discontent.

5. The American two-party system made it hard for a third party to establish itself and enabled the major parties to appropriate, at their convenience, parts of the programs advanced by reform-oriented third parties.

6. [This comes not from Sombart but from the labor historian Selig Perlman:] The massive waves of immigration led to deep ethnic cleavages within the working class, so that earlier, "native" workers rose on the social scale while newer groups of immigrants took the least desirable jobs. It therefore became extremely hard to achieve a unified class consciousness within the American working class.

Neatly bundled together, such "factors" can seem more than sufficient for explaining the distinctive political course of America. But when examined somewhat closely, these factors tend—not, of course, to disappear—but to seem less conclusive: they *are* present, some of them all the time and all of them some of the time, but their bearing upon American socialism remains, I would say, problematic.

A methodological criticism of the Sombartian approach has been made by Aileen Kraditor: that Sombart, like the Marxists, takes for granted a necessary historical course against which American experience is to be found, if not wanting, then deviant, and therefore requiring "special explanation." But it's quite likely, argues Kraditor, that no such overall historical direction can be located and that what really needs explaining is not why socialism failed in America, but why anyone thought it might succeed. Well, I am prepared to grant the dubiousness of the European model / American deviation approach, but would argue that there is some value in pursuing it tentatively, if only to see *where else* it might lead.

The Sombartian "factors" are too encompassing and thereby virtually ahistorical: they explain too much and thereby too little. They can hardly tell us why the American working class in the 1880s and 1890s engaged in very militant and even violent strikes yet did not "move ahead" to any large-scale socialist beliefs, nor can they tell us why the American socialist movement thrived, more or less, at one moment and collapsed at another. Such large historical "factors" as Sombart invokes may be overdetermining. Insofar as they apply, they leave little room for human agency, diversity, and surprise; they fall too readily into a "vulgar Marxist" assumption that human beings act exclusively or even mainly out of direct economic interest. And as a result, the problem for historians becomes to explain how *any* significant socialist movement ever did appear in this country. Between the Sombartian "factors" and the fate of a particular political movement there is, so to say, too much space; what is missing is the whole range of national culture—how people think, the myths by which they live, the impulsions that move them to action, and, not least of all, the circumstances and approaches of particular socialist movements.*

---

*"Most of the attempted [Sombartian] answers," writes Daniel Bell, "have discussed not *causes* but *conditions*. . . . An inquiry into the fate of a social movement has to be pinned to the specific questions of time, place, and opportunity. . . ."[10] Bell's distinction between "condition"

In any case, let us now glance at some of the Sombartian causes for the failure of American socialism.

Absence of a Feudal Past

This argument has been most skillfully restated by the political theorist Louis Hartz. He isolates

> three factors stemming from the European feudal inheritance, the absence of which in the United States precluded the possibility of a major socialist experience. One is a sense of class which an aristocratic culture communicates to the bourgeoisie and which both communicate to the proletariat. Another is the experience of social revolution implemented by the middle class which the proletariat also inherits. . . . Finally . . . the memory of the medieval corporate spirit which, after liberal assault, the socialist movement seeks to recreate in the form of modern collectivism.[11]

Behind Hartz's analysis there is a historical truth: that European socialist movements gained part of their following through alliances with bourgeois democratic movements in a common struggle against traditional or "feudal" institutions; and that the socialist movements kept their following by making demands

---

and "cause" is suggestive, but hard to maintain. He means, I suppose, that a condition is a relatively stable or latent circumstance that enables or disables a certain course of action—as when we say that the condition of prosperity in the 1920s made the growth of socialism unlikely. A cause is a closely operative, precipitating event—as when we say the Socialist Party's decline during and after World War I was partly caused by governmental repression. Yet I can see the Sombartians replying that if a condition is sufficiently strong and enduring, it may, in its workings, be all but indistinguishable from a cause.

that the plebes be granted political rights, promised but not fully delivered. Hartz makes much of the absence of this enabling condition in America, and, before him, Lenin had noted that America has one of "the most firmly established democratic systems, which confronts the proletariat with purely socialist tasks."[12]

In part at least, both Hartz and Lenin are wrong. For just as French socialists in the nineteenth century worked, as the Marxist phrase goes, to "fulfill the bourgeois revolution" by creating social space for the working class, and just as Chartism strove to gain for the English workers political rights within the bourgeois system, so there were in America major "democratic [as distinct from so-called purely socialist] tasks" to be undertaken by socialists and liberals. These concerned large segments of the population: for instance, the struggle for women's suffrage, in which the socialists played an important part, and the struggle for black rights, in which the socialists could have played an important part, had it not been for the sectarian Debsian claim that black freedom could be achieved "only" through socialism and consequently required no separate movement or demands. The struggle in Europe to do away with "feudal" or aristocratic hangovers has an equivalent, *mutatis mutandis,* in America as a struggle to live up to the promise of the early republic.

It's interesting that Marx and Engels could not decide whether the distinctiveness of American society was a boon or a burden for American socialism. At one point Engels, quite as if he had just read Hartz, wrote that Americans are "born conservatives—just *because* America is so purely bourgeois, so entirely without a feudal past and therefore proud of its purely bourgeois organization."[13] At another point, quite as if he had just read Hartz's critics, Engels cited "the more favorable soil of America, where no medieval ruins bar the way. . . ."[14]

The argument, then, can cut both ways. Absence of a feudal past has made for greater "civic integration," a feeling among all (except the blacks) that they "belonged." The American working class seems never quite to have regarded itself as the kind of "outsider" or pariah that the working classes of Europe once did. Whatever discontents might develop—numerous and grave in nineteenth-century America, from abolitionism to major strikes—were likely to be acted out within the flexible consensus of American myth, or as a complaint that our values had been betrayed by the plutocrats. Only the Marxists were feckless enough to attempt a head-on collision with the national myth, and what it mostly brought them was a bad headache.

But if America, in S. M. Lipset's phrase, was "a new nation" that gave its citizens a strong sense of independence and worth, then precisely this enabled them to fight staunchly for their rights. American labor strikes in the late nineteenth and early twentieth centuries were often more bloody than those in Europe. And it was, I think, two utterly divergent variants of the American myth, two simplified crystallizations at the right and left extremes, that made the class struggle so fierce in America. The capitalists, persuaded that Americans should be able to do as they wished with their property and pay whatever wages they proposed to pay, and the workers, persuaded that Americans (or Americans-in-the-making) should stand up as free men and resist exploitation, appealed to the same deeply embedded myth of the native citizen blessed with freedom by God.

There was a sharp class struggle in America during the decades after the Civil War, even without the questionable benefits of feudal hangovers, and in stressing its presence, as against those who kept talking about "classlessness," the Marxists were right. There was even a kind of class consciousness in the American working class, though this was hard to specify and the Marxists rarely succeeded in doing so, if only because it was a class consciousness that took the form, mostly, of an invocation of early republican values and a moralistic evangelicism. Sombart put the matter well: "There is expressed in the worker, as in all Americans, a boundless optimism, which comes out of a belief in the mission and greatness of his country, a belief that often has a religious tinge."[15] This belief, with its "religious tinge," could be turned toward Social Darwinism or toward unionism, populism, and early socialism.

As for Hartz's third factor—the lack of a remembered "medieval corporate spirit" which might help recreate "modern collectivism"—one may suppose that such a memory did have some influence on European workers in the mid-nineteenth century. (I suspect it has more influence on historians of romanticist inclination.) But it's hard to believe that by the 1920s or 1930s this "memory" played much of a role in the collective expression of, say, the French workers. And if Americans had no such tradition to draw upon, it would be a crude exaggeration to conclude that the only other tradition remaining to us has been an unmodulated "possessive individualism." Herbert Gutman, a historian of the American working class, has nicely distinguished between individualist and independent traditions. There are traditions of independent Americans cooperating for common ends, in everything from frontier communities to utopian colonies, from abolitionist movements to the early unions; and Gutman has further noted that the agitational literature of American unionism in the late nineteenth century echoed these very themes of the unionism of the 1830s.

It would be wrong simply to dismiss Hartz's analysis, for it speaks to commonly perceived realities and, even with all reasonable qualifications, it has an evident power. But it has to be put forward in more nuanced terms than Hartz has proposed, and this means that his now famous "factors," even if they rendered the rise of socialism in America *difficult,* do not suffice to explain its unhappy fate.

On the Reefs of Roast Beef

America, wrote Sombart, was "the promised land of capitalism," where "on the reefs of roast beef and apple pie socialistic Utopias . . . are sent to their doom."[16] This pithy sentence appears to carry a self-evident validity, but recent historical and sociological investigations create enough doubts so that, at the very least, we must qualify Sombart's conclusion.

It is an exaggeration to suggest that the American workers, or members of the lower classes, have enjoyed a steady material abundance. Large segments of the population, gasping for breath, have never reached those famous "reefs of roast beef." There is a profound truth in Nathaniel Hawthorne's remark that "in this republican country, amid the fluctuating waves of our social life, somebody is always at the drowning-point."

From the 1870s until the present we have had sharply varying times of well-being and distress, largely in accord with the cyclical character of capitalist boom and crisis; times when the standard of living rose visibly for many workers, as during World War I and the decades between 1940 and 1970; and times when, as in the last third of the nineteenth and first two decades of the twentieth centuries, certain American workers, like the building mechanics, did improve their lot while those working in mills, packing plants, and clothing factories did not. Differentiations of income and material condition among American workers have often been sharper than those in class-ridden Europe. They continue to our present moment, between skilled and/or unionized workers and that segment of the "secondary" work force consisting of ill-paid and largely unorganized blacks, Hispanics, and illegal immigrants in fugitive light industries.

Still other shadows fall across Sombart's bright picture—for example, the extent to which American workers have been subject to industrial accidents because this country, until recently, refused to pass the kind of social legislation that had long been enacted in Europe. For a good many historians it has nevertheless been the supposed objective advantages of American society when compared with European societies of the late nineteenth and early twentieth centuries—a higher standard of living, a greater degree of social mobility—that largely explain the failures of American socialism. But, as far as I have been able to gather from various historical studies, the evidence regarding standards of living and social mobility remains inconclusive. For one thing, the technical problems in making comparisons on such matters are very severe. It is hard to know exactly how to "measure" standards of living and social mobility, since so many elements of experience, some by no means readily quantifiable, enter into them.

Seymour Martin Lipset, a close observer in this area, writes that

> a number of students of social mobility in comparative perspective (Sorokin, Glass, Lipset and Bendix, Miller, Blau and Duncan, and Bourdon) have concluded from an examination of mobility data collected in various countries that the American rate of mass social mobility is not uniquely high, that a number of European countries have had comparable rates. . . .[17]

By contrast, Stephan Thernstrom, who has assembled valuable data about working-class mobility in Boston and Newburyport during the nineteenth and first two decades of the twentieth centuries, concludes that mobility was significantly higher in a big city like Boston than in a town like Newburyport, and, indeed, that in Boston "the dream of individual mobility was [not] illusory [during the nineteenth century] and that collective advance was [not] the only realistic hope for the American worker."[18]

A more recent and notably meticulous study by Peter R. Shergold comparing real wage rates and real family income in Pittsburgh, Pennsylvania, and two English cities, Birmingham and Sheffield, for the years 1899–1913, demonstrates, however, the enormous difficulties of such comparisons. Shergold concludes

> that assertions of relative American affluence must be severely qualified. Unskilled workers experienced similar levels of material welfare in Britain and the United States in the 1900s, and it is quite possible that English laborers actually enjoyed a higher standard of living during the last quarter of the nineteenth century. The dominant characteristic of the American labor force was not comparative income superiority, but the much greater inequality of wage distribution. The most highly-paid manual employees, primarily skilled workers, earned substantially larger incomes than those in equivalent English occupations, whereas low-paid workers received incomes similar to those in England. In short, the fruits of economic growth, the benefits of emergent corporate capitalism, were far more unevenly distributed among wage earners in the United States than in England.

And again:

> It is the comparative inequality of wage rewards in the United States, an income gulf widened by ethnic heterogeneity and racial prejudice, that must provide the socioeconomic context within

> which to analyze the American labor movement. American workers found it profoundly difficult to perceive their very diverse lifestyles as the product of a common exploitation. It was not a high average standard of living that dictated how they behaved. Rather, in a supreme historical paradox, it was the combination of a uniquely egalitarian ideology—"Americanism" —with extravagant inequality of material circumstances.[19]

Helpful as Shergold's material is in undermining older assertions about the "objective" reasons for the difficulties of American socialism (and, for that matter, of the American labor movement), the exact pertinence of his work remains debatable. Had he chosen to compare an American industrial city with cities in Eastern or Southern Europe, areas from which so many industrial workers in America emigrated, the economic disparities would probably have been more dramatic—and the statistical difficulties still greater—than in the work he did. In any case, his evidence that skilled workers in an American industrial city were better off than those in a similar English one may help explain the varying fates of socialism in America and England, since skilled workers played an important part in the early socialist movements.

Though the scholarly material on standards of living and social mobility is valuable—indeed, one wishes there were a good deal more—it doesn't by itself sustain Sombartian generalizations about American material conditions as the central cause of the difficulties and failures of American socialism. Even if one believes that Stephan Thernstrom's conclusions about the possibilities of individual improvement in late-nineteenth-century America probably hold for the country as a whole, the evidence is not sufficiently stark or unambiguous to form, or contribute heavily to, a *sufficient* explanation for the sharply different fates of socialism in the United States and Europe.

Nor is there any reason to believe, either from experience or research, that affluence necessarily makes for docility among workers. To argue that it does is to succumb to a crude sort of reductive economism, according to which the outlook of the worker is determined by nothing more than his personal circumstances. There has, to the contrary, been a strand of social thought that has seen extreme poverty as a demoralizing condition, likely to inhibit rather than stimulate political activism. S. M. Lipset cites the fact that "strong socialist movements exist in countries with high rates of social mobility," such as Australia and New Zealand, and Michael Harrington that the German social democracy's greatest growth occurred at a time of relative prosperity, between the 1870s and World War I. A paper by Philip Dawson and Gilbert Shapiro, following de Tocqueville's lead, shows that just before the French Revolution of 1789 those segments of the French bourgeoisie which had significantly improved their position were more vigorous in expressing opposition to the *ancien régime* than those which had not.

Studies comparing in close detail the conditions of American and European workers tend to be cautious regarding the Sombartian conclusion about "roast beef." A brilliant essay by James Holt comparing trade unions in the British and U.S. steel industries from 1880 to 1914 finds that the main factors thwarting class solidarity among the Americans were (1) the rapidity of technological advance, which reduced the need for skilled workers, who were often the most militant unionists, and (2) the ferocity of American employers, who often used brutal methods to break the unions. "The most striking difference between the two situations [American and British steel industries] concerns the behavior of employers rather than employees. In both countries, the impulse to organize was present among steelworkers but in one [Britain] most employers offered little resistance to union growth while in the other [the United States] they generally fought back vigorously." Holt concludes suggestively:

> The weakness and political conservatism of the American labor movement in the late 19th and early 20th centuries have often been seen primarily as the product of a lack of class consciousness among American workingmen. In the United States, it is suggested, class lines were more fluid and opportunities for advancement more rapid than in European countries. . . . Perhaps so, yet . . . in some ways the American workingman was more rather than less oppressed than his British counterpart. The retreat of so many American union leaders from a youthful socialism to a cautious and conservative "business unionism" may have reflected less a growing enthusiasm for the . . . status quo than a resigned acknowledgment that in a land where the propertied middle classes dominated politically and the big corporations ruled supreme in industry, accommodation was more appropriate than confrontation.[20]

Insofar as the roast-beef argument finds most American workers refusing socialism because they were relatively satisfied with their lot, it would seem to follow that, *for the same reason,* they would also reject militant class action. But many did turn to militant class or labor action. The history of American workers suggests not at all that a surfeit of good things led to passivity and acquiescence; it suggests only—and this is something very different—that the intermittent outbursts of labor militancy did not often end in socialist politics.

The Sombartian argument in its blunt form is not defensible. But to say this isn't to deny that the varying degrees of material comfort among segments of the American working class have probably constituted (to borrow a phrase from Daniel Bell) a limiting condition on the growth of American socialism. This relative or partial material comfort may help explain why American socialism was never likely to become a mass movement encompassing major segments of the working class; but it doesn't suffice for explaining something more interesting: why American socialism has had so uneven a history, with modest peaks and virtual collapse at several points.

What seems crucial is that social mobility in this country has been *perceived* differently from the way it has been perceived in Europe. The myth of opportunity for energetic individuals rests on a measure of historical actuality but also has taken on a power independent of, *even when in conflict with,* the social actuality. This myth has held the imagination of Americans across the decades, including immigrants dreadfully exploited when they came here but who apparently felt that almost anything in the New World, being new, was better than what they had known in the old. Here we enter the realm of national psychology and cultural values, which is indeed what we will increasingly have to do as we approach another of the "objective factors" commonly cited among the reasons for the failure of American socialism:

The Lure of Free Land

As it turns out, escape from onerous work conditions in the East to free land in the West was largely a myth. "In the 1860s, it took $1,000 [then a lot of money] to make a go of a farm, and the cost increased later in the century. So for every industrial worker who became a farmer twenty farmers became city dwellers. And for every free farm acquired by a farmer [under the Homestead Act of 1862], nine were purchased by railroads, speculators, or by the Government itself." There follows, however, a crucial proviso: if free land did not actually fulfill its mythic function, many people did not give up the dream that it would.[21] And perhaps, I'd add, not so much the dream of actually moving to a farm in the West as a shared feeling that the frontier and the wilderness remained powerful symbolic forces enabling Americans to find solace in the thought of escape even when they were not able to act upon it.

But is there not a contradiction between the last two of the Sombartian "objective factors"? If the American worker felt so contented with his life as the roast-beef-and-apple-pie argument suggests, why should he have wanted to escape from it to the rigors of pioneering on the American prairie? This question—the force of which is hardly diminished by the fact that not many workers actually did set out for the West—was asked by the German Social Democratic paper *Vorwärts* when it came to review Sombart's book:

> ... Why under such circumstances [does] the American worker "escape into freedom" ... that is, withdraw from the hubbub of capitalism, by settling on hitherto uncultivated land [?] If capitalism is so good to him, he could not help but feel extraordinarily well-off under its sceptre.... There is clearly a glaring contradiction here.[22]

The lure of the frontier, the myth of the West surely held a strong grip on the imaginations of many Americans during the late nineenth century—and later too. But it soon became an independent power quite apart from any role the West may actually have played as a "safety valve" for urban discontent.

You have surely noticed the direction my argument is taking: away from a stress upon material conditions (even while acknowledging that in the last analysis they may well have constituted a large barrier to socialist growth) and toward a focusing on the immediate problems of American socialists that were or are in part open to solution through an exertion of human intelligence and will. Let me mention two: large-scale immigration, which created ethnic divisions within the working class, and the distinctive political structure of the United States.

The Immigrant Problem

The rise of American socialism in the late nineteenth and early twentieth centuries coincides with the greatest wave of immigration this country has ever experienced, an immigration drawn largely from Eastern and Southern Europe, with large numbers of Italians, Slavs, Jews, and Poles. When a nonspecialist looks into the historical literature, the main conclusion to be drawn is that it would be foolhardy to draw any large conclusions. Or, if pressed, I would say that the waves of the "new immigrants"—the more poorly educated, largely peasant stock from premodern countries—presented more of a problem to the American *unions* than to the socialists.

Many immigrants in this "second wave" came with a strong desire to work hard, save money, and go back home; they thought of themselves as what we'd call "guest workers," and that is one reason many came without their wives. The rate of return among East Europeans and Italians was very high. Between 1908 and 1910, for South and East Europeans, forty-four out of a hundred who came went back; between 1907 and 1911, for Italians, seventy-three out of a hundred who came went back. Such people were not likely to be attracted to political movements, especially those that might get them in trouble with the authorities or might interfere with their projects for self-exploitation as workers; nor, for the same reasons, were these immigrants often good material for unionization, though a study by Victor Greene has shown that the Slavs in western Pennsylvania, if conditions grew desperate enough, could be recruited as strong supporters of strike actions. As Jerome Karabel has shrewdly remarked: "If . . . a 'safety valve' did indeed exist for the discontented American worker, it was apparently to be found less on the frontier than in tired old Europe."[23]

Upon arrival, South and East European immigrants often took the worst jobs. Usually without industrial skills, these people were shunted to brute labor, on the railroads and in the steel mills. Their presence enabled the "first wave" of immigrants, from Northern Europe, to rise on the social scale and, above these, the native-born to enter new supervisory posts created by a rapid industrial expansion. The American working class was thereby split into competing ethnic segments—and the contempt native-born and earlier immigrants often showed the newer immigrants did nothing to heal this split. No matter what the Marxist schema might propose, these ethnic divisions were often felt more strongly than any hypothetical class consciousness, except perhaps during strikes, in which a momentary solidarity could be achieved.

Partly in reaction to the ethnic and racial antagonisms they met from other workers, but partly from a natural desire to live with those who spoke the same language, ate the same foods, and shared the same customs, many immigrant workers huddled into ethnic neighborhoods, miniature strongholds in which to beat off the contempt of their "betters." These neighborhoods could often be controlled by shrewd politicians offering practical advice and social help; among the Italians, for instance, by *padroni* doubling as labor contractors in the construction industry. This heavy concentration in ethnic neighborhoods usually made for political conservatism and obviously served to thwart class or political consciousness. Later students would see such neighborhoods as enclaves of parochial narrowness or as communities enabling their members to accumulate strength for a move into the larger American world—obviously they could be both. Recently a more sophisticated analysis, by Ira Katznelson and others, has made much of the split between the immigrant as worker in the plant and as resident in the ethnic community, sometimes able to achieve an intense militancy in bitter economic struggles against employers, yet docile in relation to the conservative leadership of the ethnic neighborhood.

Harsh as the exploitation of immigrant workers often was, many of them retained a stubborn conviction that if they accepted deprivation in the short run, their lot would ultimately be bettered—or at least that of their children would be. Certain immigrant groups, especially the Jews, staked almost everything on the educational opportunities offered by America. Often accompanied by desperate homesickness for the old country and harsh curses for the crudity of life in America, the promise of the New World nevertheless gripped the imagination of the immigrants. American radicals might point to real injustices, but to newcomers who had left behind autocratic and caste-ridden nations, our easy manners and common acceptance of democratic norms could seem wonderfully attractive. And there is a psychological point to be added: it was hard enough to be a Slav in Pittsburgh or a Pole in Chicago without the additional burden of that "anti-Americanism" with which the socialists were often charged.

Much of the "new immigration" consisted of Catholics, people still close to the faith, in whom a suspicion of socialism had been implanted by a strongly conservative clergy. The labor historian Selig Perlman believed that the immigrant character of American labor was a major reason for the difficulties of the socialists: "American labor remains one of the most heterogeneous laboring classes in existence. . . . With a working class of such composition, to make socialism . . . the official 'ism' of the movement, would mean . . . deliberately driving the Catholics . . . out of the labor movement. . . .[24]

Now, Perlman's point seems beyond dispute if taken simply as an explanation of why socialism could not, or should not, have become the dominant outlook of the American labor movement. But it does not explain very much about socialist fortunes in general—unless, of course, you assume that domination of the AFL was the crucial requirement for socialist success in America. That such domination would have helped the socialists is obvious; but it's not at all obvious that, lacking it, they were doomed to extinction or mere sect existence. In truth, the socialists had plenty of possibilities for recruitment within the country at large before they could so much as reach the new immigrants.

Nor should it be supposed that the immigrants formed a solid conservative mass. In the Debsian era, socialist strength was centered in a number of immigrant communities: the Germans, the Jews, and the Finns, all of whom clustered in ethnic neighborhoods that some recent analysts have seen as bulwarks of conservatism. As if to illustrate how the same data can be used for sharply opposing claims, one historian, John Laslett, has argued that it was the "process of ethnic assimilation" rather than ethnic isolation that hindered the socialists:

> This is perhaps clearest in the case of the Brewery Workers Union, whose socialism may in large part be ascribed to the

> influences of socialists who came to this country after the abortive German revolution of 1848, and in greater numbers after Bismarck's antisocialist legislation of 1878. The radicalism of the union noticeably declined as these older groups either died off, moved upward into the entrepreneurial or professional middle class, or were replaced by ethnic groups whose commitment to socialism was less intense.[25]

The immigrants, to be sure, presented practical and moral-political problems for the socialists. Many immigrants, even if friendly to the movement, could not vote, nor did they rush to acquire citizenship. There were segments of the party that harbored disgraceful antiforeign sentiments, and this led to internecine disputes. The plethora of immigrant communities made for difficulties: Morris Hillquit once noted ruefully that the party had to put out propaganda in twenty different languages. For a union trying to organize, say, a steel plant in Pittsburgh, where the work force was split ethnically and linguistically, this could be a devastating problem. For the socialists, however, it would have been crucial only if they had had much of a chance of reaching many of these "new immigrants," or if they had already scored such successes among the indigenous American population that all that remained in their way was the recalcitrance of immigrant workers. Such, obviously, was not the case. No; the argument from the divisive consequences of immigration does not take us very far in explaining the difficulties of American socialism.

It is when we reach the last of our "objective factors,"

The American Political System

that we come closer to the actual difficulties socialists encountered in America.

If the authors of the Constitution had in mind to establish a political system favoring a moderately conservative two-party structure—a kind of "centrism" allowing some flexibility within a stable consensus politics but also putting strong barriers in the way of its principled critics—then they succeeded brilliantly. Our shrewdly designed system combines a great deal of rigidity in its governing structure with a great deal of flexibility in its major parties. Our method of electing presidents requires that the parties be inclusive enough to cement political coalitions before Election Day, and that means bargaining and compromise, which blur political and ideological lines. Our method of governing, however, makes for a continuity of elites, tends to give the political center an overwhelming preponderance, and makes it tremendously difficult for insurgent constituencies to achieve political strength unless they submit to the limits of one of the major parties. In recent years, this peculiar mixture of rigidity and flexibility has, if anything, become more prevalent. The tremendous costliness of running for political office, now that television has largely replaced the public meeting and advertising slogans the political oration, makes it all but impossible for minority parties to compete. It also enables rich men—noble, eccentric, and wicked—to take on an excessive role in political life. Yet the growth of the primary system and the fact that most voters pay even less attention to primaries than to elections means that coherent minorities can often achieve their ends through cleverness and concentration.

There are theorists by the dozen who regard all this as a master stroke in behalf of maintaining democracy. Perhaps they are right. At least, they may be right if the society does not have to confront major crises, as during the immediate pre–Civil War years and the Depression era, when the political system comes under severe strain. But if the system helps maintain democracy, it also seriously disables democratic critics of capitalism.

For the most part, all of this constitutes the common coin of American political science. Let me therefore try to sharpen the focus by discussing the problem from the point of view of the socialist movement as it kept trying to establish itself in the country's political life.

One of my most wearying memories, when I think back to years in various socialist groups, is that of efforts we would make to get on the ballot. Most states had rigid requirements, sometimes mere rigged handicaps, for minor parties. In New York State you had to obtain a certain number of qualified signatures from all the counties, and this would mean sending volunteers to upstate rural communities where signators ready to help socialists were pretty rare. In Ohio during the 1930s the number of required signatures, as I recall, was outrageously high. Well, we would throw ourselves into the effort of collecting signatures, and then have to face a court challenge from a major party, usually the more liberal one, since it had more to lose from our presence on the ballot than the conservatives. (It's amusing how often Republicans turned out to be staunch "defenders" of minority rights. . . .) If, finally, we did get on the ballot, we were often so exhausted that there was little or no energy, to say nothing of money, left for the actual campaign.

Over and over again the socialists would face this problem: friendly people would come up to our candidates—especially Norman Thomas—and say they agreed with our views but would nevertheless vote for "the lesser evil" because they didn't "want to throw away their vote." We tried to scorn such sentiments, but, given the American political system, especially the zero-sum game for presidential elections, there really was a core of sense in what these people said.

One of the few occasions when the socialist vote was relatively large—in 1912, when the party drew 6 percent of the vote—is partly explained by the fact that, as Thomas put it, "voters that year were pretty sure that the winner would be either Woodrow Wilson or Theodore Roosevelt, not William H. Taft, and they didn't believe that the difference between these two fairly progressive men was important enough to prevent their voting for their real preference," the socialist Eugene Debs. I'd guess Thomas was right when he added that if America had had "a parliamentary rather than a presidential government, we should have had, under some name or other, a moderately strong socialist party."

The idea of a long-range *political* movement slowly accumulating strength for some ultimate purpose has simply not appealed to the American imagination. Movements outside the political process, yes—from abolitionism to feminism, from municipal reform to civil rights. But let the supporters of these movements enter electoral politics, and the expectation becomes one of quick victory. S. M. Lipset has described this phenomenon:

> . . . Extra-party "movements" arise for moralistic causes, which are initially not electorally palatable. Such movements are not doomed to isolation and inefficacy. If mainstream political leaders recognize that a significant segment of the electorate feels alienated . . . , they will readapt one of the major party coalitions. But in so doing, they temper much of the extremist moralistic fervor. . . . The protestors are absorbed into a major party coalition, but, like the abolitionists who joined the Republicans, the Populists who merged with the Democrats, or the radicals who backed the New Deal, they contribute to the policy orientation of the newly formed coalition.[26]

To which I need only add a clever observation Sombart made in 1906, which is still, I suspect, largely true:

> It is an unbearable feeling for an American to belong to a party that always and forever comes out of the election with small figures. . . . A member of a minority party finds himself on election day . . . compelled to stand at one side with martyr-like resignation—something which in no way accords with the American temperament.[27]

At least a significant number of Americans have never hesitated to "stand at one side with a martyr-like resignation" or even with rage in behalf of moral causes. But, curiously, this has not seemed to extend to the electoral system: *there* they have to strike it rich. That may be one reason they sometimes strike it so poor.

The search for answers often leads to nothing more than a redefining of questions. To discount but not dismiss the customary "objective factors" cited as explanations for the failure of American socialism is by no means to reject the idea of "American exceptionalism," namely, that conditions in the United States have differed crucially from the Marxist model for the development of capitalism and/or the way capitalism actually developed in Europe. It is, rather, to transfer our explanatory stress from material conditions to the character of American culture. Exceptionalism among us took primarily an ideological or a mythic form, a devotion to the idea that this country could be exempt from the historical burdens that had overwhelmed Europe. It seems obvious that so distinctive a culture, defining itself through an opposition to, even a rejection of, Europe, cannot finally be understood apart from the shaping context of special historical circumstances: it did not arise merely as an idea in someone's head, or an Idea in a Collective Head. Yet I want to stress the independent power, the all-but-autonomous life, of the American myth and its remarkable persistence, despite enormous changes in social conditions. The ideology or myth—call it what you will, as long as you keep your eye fixed on Gatsby's "green light"—seems *almost* impervious to the modifying pressures of circumstance. It isn't, of course; but what strikes one is the extent to which it continues, in good circumstances and bad, to shape our imagination.

What is this myth? It consists in a shared persuasion, often penetrating deeper into our consciousness than mere language can express, that America is the home of a people shaped by or at least sharing in Providence. America is the land of the settler's paradisial wilderness, the setting of the Puritan's New Israel. America is humanity's second chance. Such sentiments rest on a belief that we have already had our revolution and it was led by George Washington, so that appeals for another one are superfluous and malicious, or that, for the millions who came here from Europe in the last 150 years, the very act of coming constituted a kind of revolution.

That many Americans have found it entirely possible to yield to this myth while simultaneously attacking our socioeconomic institutions, or complaining bitterly that the slaveocracy disgraced us, the plutocrats stole our inheritance, Wall Street fleeced us, the capitalists exploited us, and the military-industrial complex sent our sons to death—all this seems clear. To a simple rationalist or vulgar Marxist, the ability to hold at once to the animating myth behind the founding of America and the most bitter criticism of its violation or abandonment or betrayal, may seem a contradiction; but if so, it is precisely from such contradictions that our collective existence has been formed.

The distinctive American ideology takes on a decidedly nonideological mask. I call it, very roughly, Emersonianism, though I know it had its sources in American and indeed European thought long before Emerson. By now, of course, "Emersonianism" has become as elusive and protean a category as Marxism or Freudianism. What I mean to suggest is that Emerson, in a restatement of an old Christian heresy, raised the *I* to semidivine status, thereby providing a religious sanction for the American cult of individualism. Traditional Christianity had seen man as a being like God, but now he was to be seen as one sharing, through osmosis with the oversoul, directly in the substance of divinity. This provided a new vision of man for a culture proposing to define itself as his new home—provided that vision by insisting that man be regarded as a self-creating and self-sufficient being fulfilled through his unmediated relation to nature and God. The traditional European view that human beings are in good measure defined or described through social characteristics and conditions was, at least theoretically, discounted; the new American, singing songs of himself, would create himself through spontaneous assertions, which might at best graze sublimity and at worst drop to egoism. The American, generically considered, could make his fate through will and intuition, a self-induced grace.

Now, this vision can be employed in behalf of a wide range of purposes—myth is always promiscuous. It can show forth the Emerson who, in behalf of "a perfect unfolding of individual nature," brilliantly analyzed human alienation in a commercial society, attacking the invasion of "Nature by Trade . . . [as it threatened] to upset the balance of man, and establish a new, universal Monarchy more tyrannical than Babylon or Rome." And it can emerge in the Emerson who told his countrymen that "money . . . is in its effects and laws as beautiful as roses. Property keeps the accounts of the world, and is always moral."

This American vision can be turned toward the authoritarian

monomania of Captain Ahab or to the easy fraternity of Ishmael and Queequeg. It can coexist with Daniel Webster and inspire Wendell Phillips. It can be exploited by Social Darwinism and sustain the abolitionists. It can harden into a nasty individualism and yield to the mass conformity de Tocqueville dreaded. Arising from the deepest recesses of the American imagination, it resembles Freud's description of dreams as showing "a special tendency to reduce two opposites to a unity or to represent them as one thing." No one has to like this vision, but anyone trying to cope with American experience had better acknowledge its power.

This complex of myth and ideology, sentiment and prejudice, for which I use "Emersonianism" as a convenient label, forms the ground of "American exceptionalism." Politically it has often taken the guise of a querulous antistatism, at times regarded as a native absolute—though that seldom kept many people from aligning it with the demands of big business for government subsidies. It can veer toward an American version of anarchism, suspicious of all laws, forms, and regulations, asserting a fraternity of two, sometimes even one, against all communal structures. Tilt toward the right and you have the worship of "the free market"; tilt toward the left and you have the moralism of American reformers, even the syndicalism of the IWW. Snakelike, this "Emersonianism" can also subside into or next to the Lockean moderation of the American Constitution and political arrangement. ("The American Whig leaders" of the postrevolutionary period, Sacvan Bercovitch shrewdly remarks, "brought the violence of revolution under control by making revolution a controlling metaphor of national identity.")

It is notable that most nineteenth-century critics of American society appealed to the standards—violated, they said—of the early republic. They did this not as a tactical device but out of sincere conviction. "We will take up the ball of the Revolution where our fathers dropped it," declared the agrarian radicals of the New York anti-rent movement, "and roll it to the final consummation of freedom and independence of the Masses." The social historian Herbert Gutman finds the same rhetoric in the propaganda of the late-nineteenth-century trade unions. And Sacvan Bercovitch finds it in the declarations of a large number of American radicals throughout that century:

> William Lloyd Garrison organized the American Anti-Slavery Society as "a renewal of the nation's founding principles" and of "the national ideal." Frederick Douglass based his demands for black liberation on America's "destiny" . . . and "the genius of American institutions. . . ." As a leading historian of the period has remarked: ". . . the typical reformer, for all his uncompromising spirit, was no more alienated—no more truly rebellious—than the typical democrat. . . . He might sound radical while nevertheless associating himself with the fundamental principles and underlying tendencies of America."[28]

It's a pity that our indigenous nineteenth-century radicalism had largely exhausted itself by the time small socialist groups, mostly immigrant in composition, began to be organized in the 1880s—or at least could not find a point of significant relation with them. The abolitionist Wendell Phillips began with a pure Emersonian invocation: ". . . We are bullied by institutions. . . . Stand on the pedestal of your own individual independence, summon these institutions about you, and judge them." Once the fight against slavery was won, Phillips moved ahead to other causes, warning against "the incoming flood of the power of incorporated wealth" and calling—in a political style Richard Hofstadter has described as "Yankee homespun" socialism—for an "equalization of property."[29] He became—almost—a bridge between nineteenth-century radicalism and the new American socialism. And like other American dissenters, he held fast to the tradition of invoking the principles of the republic—principles, he said, that had been violated and betrayed.

Recognizing the power of this traditional response is by no means to acquiesce in the delusions that have often been justified in its name. It isn't, for example, to acquiesce in the delusion that America has been or is a "classless" society. Or that there has been any lack among us of bloody battles between capital and labor. Or that there are not today, as in the past, glaring injustices that call for remedy. To recognize the power of the American myth of a covenant blessing the new land is simply to recognize a crucial fact in our history—and one that seems to me at least as decisive for the fate of socialism in this country as the material conditions that are usually cited.

If you go through the writings of American socialists you can find glimmerings and half-recognitions that they have had to function in a culture ill-attuned to their fundamental outlook. The keenest statements on this matter come from an odd pair: an Italian Marxist, Antonio Gramsci, who had no direct contact with America, and an American radical of the 1930s, Leon Samson, remembered only by historians who make the left their specialty. In his *Notebooks* Gramsci writes:

> The Anglo-Saxon immigrants are themselves an intellectual, but more especially a moral, elite. . . . They import into America . . . apart from moral energy and energy of will, a certain level of civilization, a certain stage of European historical evolution, which, when transplanted by such men into the virgin soil of America, continues to develop the forces implicit in its nature. . . .[30]

In isolation, this passage could almost be taken for a rhapsody celebrating American culture; but Gramsci was a Marxist, and he proceeded to argue that the elements of uniqueness he found in the American past had reached their fulfillment in an apogee of pure capitalism, what he calls "Fordism," an unprecedented rationalization of production setting America apart from the kinds of capitalism known in Europe.

Leon Samson, a maverick socialist of the 1930s, developed a linked notion, that "Americanism" can be seen as a "substitute socialism":

> Like socialism, Americanism is looked upon . . . as a . . . platonic, impersonal attraction toward a system of ideas, a solemn assent to a handful of final notions—democracy, liberty, opportunity, to all of which the American adheres rationalistically much as a socialist adheres to his socialism—because it does him good, because it gives him work, because, so he thinks, it guarantees his happiness. . . . Every concept in socialism has its substitutive counter-concept in Americanism, and that is why the socialist argument falls so fruitlessly on the American ear. . . .[31]

Both Gramsci and Samson were shrewd enough to locate their "exceptionalism" in the mythic depths of our collective imagination, among the inner vibrations of our culture. What one may conclude from their perceptions, as perhaps from my own discussion, is that if socialism is ever to become a major force in America it must either enter deadly combat with and destroy the covenant myth or must look for some way of making its vision of the good society seem a fulfillment of that myth. Both are difficult propositions, but I need hardly say which is the less so.

Many socialists have grasped for intuitions along these lines, but have feared perhaps to articulate them, since they seemed to suggest that so impalpable a thing as a culture can have a greater power of influence than industrial structures, levels of production, and standards of living. And that may explain why many American socialists, including the intelligent ones, found it safer to retreat into the comforts of the Marxist system, with its claims to universal applicability and certain fulfillment.

Would a developed recognition of the problem as I have sketched it here have brought any large or immediate success to American socialism over the past five or six decades? Probably not. All that such a recognition might have done—all!—is to endow the American socialists with a certain independence of mind and a freedom from ideological rigidity.

So, again, we restate our central question. Not "Why is there no socialism in America?" There never was a chance for major socialist victory in this society, this culture. The really interesting question is "Why could we not build a *significant* socialist movement that would have a sustained influence?" One answer, of course, is that the kind of culture I've sketched here makes it almost impossible for a significant minority party to survive for very long. In America, politics, like everything else, tends to be all or nothing. But whether it might yet be possible for a significant minority movement to survive—one that would be political in a broad, educative sense without entangling itself in hopeless electoral efforts—is another question.

Some Inconclusive Conclusions

1. The analyses and speculations in this book apply mainly to the earlier decades of the century, into the years just before World War II. But the troubles of American—and not only American—socialism in the decades since the thirties must be located in a more terrible—indeed, an apocalyptic—setting. The

triumph of Hitlerism called into question a good many traditional assumptions of progress and schemes for human self-determination—called into question the very enterprise of mankind. The rise of Stalinism, a kind of grotesque "double" of the socialist hope, led to the destruction of entire generations, the disillusionment of hundreds of thousands of committed people, the besmirching of the socialist idea itself. As a consequence of the problems thrown up by Hitlerism and Stalinism, there has occurred an inner crisis of belief, a coming-apart of socialist thought. If we consider the crisis of socialism on an international scale within the last fifty years, then clearly these developments count at least as much as, and probably more than, the indigenous American factors I have discussed here.

2. There is a school of opinion that holds that American socialism did not fail, but succeeded insofar as it prepared the way, advanced ideas, and trained leaders for mainstream movements of labor, liberalism, etc. This view has an obvious element of truth, perhaps even consolation. Still, no one could be expected to endure the grueling effort to build a socialist movement simply so that it might serve as a "prep school" for other movements. Our final judgment must be more stringent, harder on ourselves: insofar as American socialism proposed ends distinctively its own, it did not succeed.

3. There is a more sophisticated argument about the fate of American socialism: that finally it did not matter. Europe, with its strong socialist and social-democratic movements, did not achieve democratic socialism; it could reach only the welfare state. The United States, without a major socialist movement, has also reached a welfare state, if at the moment one that is somewhat broken-down. Hence, this argument goes, what does it matter whether or not we have a socialist movement here? I

would respond that, largely because of the strength of European socialism, the welfare state in Western Europe has advanced significantly beyond that of the United States, and that there are groups within European socialism, especially in Sweden and France, that now see a need to move "beyond" the welfare state. The presence of these groups has been made possible by the continuing strength of the socialist movement in those countries.

4. The usual "objective" socioeconomic factors cited as explanations for the difficulties of American socialism are, in my judgment, genuine constraints. But I believe that the distinctiveness of American culture has played the more decisive part in thwarting socialist fortunes. And even after both kinds of reasons —the socioeconomic and the cultural—are taken into account, there remains an important margin with regard to intelligence or obtuseness, correct or mistaken strategies, which helped to determine whether American socialism was to be a measurable force or an isolated sect. That the American socialist movement must take upon itself a considerable portion of the responsibility for its failures, I have tried to show in earlier chapters.

5. In the United States, socialist movements have usually thrived during times of liberal upswing. They have hastened their own destruction whenever they have pitted themselves head-on against liberalism. If there is any future for socialism in America, it is through declaring itself to be the partial ally of a liberalism with which it shares fundamental democratic values and agrees upon certain immediate objectives; after that, it can be said that socialists propose to extend and thereby fulfill traditional liberal goals by moving toward a democratization of economic and social life. If some liberals express agreement with that perspective, then all the better.

6. American socialism has suffered from a deep-grained sectari-

anism, in part a result of the natural inclination of small groups to huddle self-protectively in their loneliness, and in part, especially during the two or three decades after 1917, a result of the baneful influence of Bolshevism. At least as important have been the fundamentalist, evangelical, and deeply antipolitical impulses rooted in our religious and cultural past, impulses that helped to shape the socialist movements in the times of Debs and Thomas far more than their participants recognized. A damaging aspect of this sectarianism was a tendency to settle into postures of righteous moral witness, to the disadvantage of mundane politics.

During its peak moments American socialism tried to combine two roles—that of moral protest and that of political reform—which in America had traditionally been largely separate, and which our political arrangements make it very difficult to unite. In principle, a socialist movement ought to fulfill both of these roles: moral protest largely beyond the political process, and social reform largely within it. A strong argument could be made that the two roles are, or should be, mutually reinforcing, with the one providing moral luster and the other practical effectiveness. But it would take an extraordinary set of circumstances (say, the moment when abolitionism flourished or the moment when the protest against the Vietnam war reached its peak) for a movement in this country to combine the two roles successfully. And what's more, it would take a movement with a degree of sophistication and flexibility that has rarely been available on the left, or anywhere else along the political spectrum.

Still, no socialist movement, if it is to maintain the integrity of its persuasions, can forgo some effort to be both the voice of protest and the agency of reform. It's not a matter of choosing between the roles of moral witness and political actor. It's a matter of finding ways through which to link properly the utopian moralism of the protester with the political realism of the activist; to ensure that the voice of high rectitude will reinforce and give breadth to the daily murmur of the reformer; to adapt to the realities of the American political system without succumbing to a small-souled pragmatism or a hermetic moralism. In some large parties, loosely and democratically structured, this has sometimes been possible, as in the British Labour Party during its best years. In a small party, such as the American Socialist Party even during its best years, this has been almost impossible.

Whether some such alliance of forces or union of impulses might still be created in America is very much a question. I do not know, but think it a project worthy of serious people.

Henry James once said that being an American is a complex fate. We American socialists could add: He didn't know the half of it.

PART TWO

The Socialist Idea

Socialism and Liberalism: Articles of Conciliation?

It will surprise no one to learn that after a reasonably diligent search I have not been able to find a serious attempt systematically to gather the usual socialist criticisms of liberalism. These criticisms, though familiar enough, appear in the literature mainly through occasional passages, unquestioned references, rude dismissals, and, in recent decades, a few wistful beckonings for reconciliation.

In the socialist literature, though not there alone, liberalism has taken on at least the following roles and meanings:

1. Especially in Europe, liberalism has signified those movements and currents of opinion that arose toward the end of the eighteenth century, seeking to loosen the constraints traditional societies had imposed on the commercial classes and proposing modes of government in which the political and economic behavior of individuals would be subjected to a minimum of regulation. Social life came to be seen as a field in which an equilibrium of desired goods could be realized if individuals were left free to

pursue their interests.* This, roughly, is what liberalism has signified in Marxist literature, starting with Marx's articles for the *Rheinische Zeitung* and extending through the polemics of Kautsky, Bernstein, and Luxemburg. In short: "classical" liberalism.

2. Both in Europe and America, liberalism has also been seen as a system of beliefs stressing such political freedoms as those specified in the U.S. Bill of Rights. Rising from lowlands of interest to plateaus of value, this view of liberalism proposes a commitment to "formal" freedoms—speech, assembly, press, etc. —so that in principle, as sometimes in practice, liberalism need have no necessary connection with or dependence upon any particular way of organizing the economy.

3. Especially in twentieth-century America but also in Europe, liberalism has come to signify movements of social reform seeking to "humanize" industrial-capitalist society, usually on the premise that this could be done sufficiently or satisfactorily without having to resort to radical/socialist measures—in current shorthand: the welfare state. At its best, this social liberalism has also viewed itself as strictly committed to the political liberalism of (2) above.

4. In America, sometimes to the bewilderment of Europeans, liberalism has repeatedly taken on indigenous traits that render it, at one extreme, virtually asocial and anarchic and, at the other extreme, virtually chiliastic and authoritarian. Perhaps because the assumptions of a liberal polity were so widely shared in nineteenth-century America (the slaveocracy apart), "liberal" as

---

*The philosophical underpinning is provided by Kant: "Everyone is entitled to seek happiness in whatever manner seems best to him, provided that he does not interfere with the freedom of others to strike toward the same objective, which can coexist with the freedom of everyone else under a conceivable general law."

a term of political designation can hardly be found in its writings. Even when liberalism as a distinctive modern politics or ideological current begins to emerge in America—first through the high-minded reforming individualism of E. L. Godkin, editor of the *Nation* during the 1880s and 1890s, and then through the socialist-nationalist progressivism of Herbert Croly, editor of *The New Republic* when it was founded in 1914—it cannot escape a heritage of native individualism, utopianism, and "conscience politics." Nor can it escape the paradisial vision that is deeply lodged in the American imagination, or a heritage of Protestant self-scrutiny, self-reliance, and self-salvation. Consequently, American liberalism has within it a strand of deep if implicit hostility toward politics *per se*—a powerful kind of moral absolutism, celebrating conscience above community, which forms both its glory and its curse.

5. Meanwhile, through the decades, liberalism has encompassed a *Weltanschauung,* a distinctive way of regarding the human situation. Despite some recent attempts to render it profound through a gloomy chiaroscuro, liberalism has customarily been dependent on that view of man which stresses rationality, good nature, optimism, and even "perfectibility" (whatever that may mean). Whether or not there is a necessary clash between the Christian and liberal views of man, and despite some strains of continuity that may coexist along with the differences, there can hardly be any question that historically, in its effort to gain its own space, liberalism has emerged as a competitor to traditional religious outlooks.

2.

That there are other significant uses of the term "liberalism" I do not doubt; but these should be quite enough. Let me note some

—by no means all—of the major socialist criticisms of the major variants of liberalism.

The socialist criticism of "classical" liberalism (joined at points by that of conservative iconoclasts like Carlyle) seems by now to have been largely absorbed in our political culture—with the exception of such ideological eccentrics as Ayn Rand and Milton Friedman. That the historical conditions of early capitalist society made a mockery of any notion of free and equal competitors entering into free and equal exchange, with each employing his gifts and taking his risks; that large masses of people were excluded from the very possibility of significant social choice; that even "liberal" governments never quite practiced the noninterventionist principles of "classical" liberalism but in fact were actively engaged in furthering the growth of bourgeois economy; that the notion of "entitlement," with its premise of some early point of fair beginnings, is too often no more than ideological—these have been the kinds of criticisms that socialists, and especially Marxists, have made of early liberalism.* The very

---

*In *Capital,* I, chap. 6 ("The Buying and Selling of Labor-Power"), Marx applies his powers of sarcasm to such assumptions of "classical" liberalism: "The sphere of circulation and exchange of commodities within which labor is bought and sold was in reality a paradise of innate human rights—governed entirely by freedom, equality, property, and Bentham. Freedom: Because the buyers and sellers of a commodity, such as labor-power, are constrained only according to their own free will. They enter into a contract as free and legally equal free agents. The contract is the final result in which their common free will is given common legal expression. Equality: Because their relationships with one another are purely those of the owners of commodities and they exchange like for like. Property: Because each individual makes use

world we live in—irreversible if inconvenient, and open to almost every mode of criticism except nostalgia for the alleged bliss of an early pure capitalism—testifies to the cogency of these criticisms.

Yet that is by no means the whole story. One of the strengths of Marxist historiography (I shall come to weaknesses) has been that even while assaulting capitalism it saw the vitality of its early phases, and that even in the course of ridiculing "classical" liberalism as an ideological rationale for bourgeois ascendancy, it honored its early liberating role in behalf of humanity at large. The early Marx—he who could write that "laws are positive and lucid universal norms in which freedom has attained an impersonal, theoretical existence independent of any arbitrary individual. A statute book is the people's Bible of freedom,"[1] or he who could write that "without parties there is no development, without division, no progress"—this early Marx clearly recognized his ties to, or descent from, the liberalism he subjected to harsh attack and sought to "transcend."

Socialists—let us be honest: some socialists—have recognized that in its heroic phase liberalism constituted one of the two or three greatest revolutionary experiences in human history. The very idea of "the self" or "the individual," quintessential to

---

only of what belongs to him. Bentham: Because each of the two thinks only of himself. The only power that holds them together and establishes a relationship between them is their egotism, personal advantage, and private interest. And precisely because each individual thinks of himself and never of anyone else, they all work toward their mutual advantage, the general good and common interest, in accordance with a preestablished harmony of things or under the auspices of a cunning knowing providence."

modern thought and sensibility, simply could not have come into being without the fructifying presence of liberalism. The liberalism that appears in eighteenth-century Europe promises a dismissal of intolerable restraints; speaks for previously unimagined rights; declares standards of sincerity and candor; offers the vision that each man will have his voice and each voice will be heard. It would be making things too easy to say that socialism emerges unambiguously out of this tradition. Obviously, there have been authoritarian alloys in the socialist metals; but when the socialist imagination is at its most serious, it proposes a dialectical relationship with "classical" liberalism: on the one hand, a refusal, of quasi-Benthamite rationales for laissez-faire economics, and, on the other, a pact in behalf of enlarging the boundaries of political freedom.

Both in some early efforts at Marxist scholarship and in recent academic revivals, socialists have charged against liberalism that its defenders elevate it to a suprahistorical abstraction, an absolute value presumably untainted by grubby interests or bloodied corruptions, whereas in actuality liberalism, like all other modes of politics, arose as a historically conditioned and thereby contaminated phenomenon, and must be regarded as susceptible to historical decay and supersession.

Now, if we see this matter mainly as one of historiography, there is a point to the socialist criticism. No political movement, not even liberalism, likes to have the time of its origins deglamorized, yet there is sufficient reason for subjecting all movements to that chastening procedure. But with regard to a living politics, this criticism is dangerous and has done a share of mischief.

The tendency of some Marxists to regard liberal ideas as mainly or merely epiphenomena of a historical movement always runs the risk of declining into an extreme relativism, that is, a historicism which acknowledges no fixed point of premise other than its own strategies of deflation. A sophisticated analogue is the "sociology of knowledge"; a vulgar reduction, the habit of speaking about "*mere* bourgeois democracy." This mode of historical analysis ignores the possibility that even movements and currents of thought conditioned by class interests can yield ideas, traditions, methods, customs that will seem of permanent value to future generations. There may not be unimpeded progress in history, but there do seem to be a few permanent conquests. To show that the principles of a liberal polity did not descend from Mount Sinai but arose together with social classes whose dominance we would like to see ended or curtailed is not at all to deny that those liberal principles are precious both to newly ascending classes and to humanity at large. To show that the Founding Fathers of the United States represented commercial interests or kept slaves or, when in office, violated some of their own precepts is not at all to diminish the value of the Bill of Rights for people who despise commercial interests, abhor slavery, and propose, if in power, never to violate their own precepts. Criticism of Jefferson's inadequacies is helped by the adequacy of Jeffersonian principles.

If these remarks seem obvious, we might remember that the history of twentieth-century politics, as also that of the twentieth-century intelligentsia, offers scant ground for resting securely in common devotion to liberal values. Quite the contrary. We are living through a century in which the liberal conquests of the nineteenth century, inadequate as these might have been, have been systematically destroyed by left and right authoritarian dictatorships. "Vulgar Marxism," with its quick reduction of ideas to ideology and its glib ascription of ideology to interest, has become the mental habit of lazy and half-educated people throughout the world.* In general, we ought to be extremely wary of all statements featuring the word "really"—as in "Mill's ideas really represent the interests of the British, etc., etc." and "Freud's ideas really reflect the condition of the Viennese, etc., etc."

Insofar, then, as the socialist criticism of liberalism has furthered an element of historical reductionism—unavoidable, I suspect, in the context of a mass movement—it has weakened the otherwise valid insistence that liberalism be treated as part of mundane history and thereby subject to mundane complications.

A powerful socialist criticism of liberalism has been that it has detached political thought and practice from shared, material life, cutting politics off from the interplay of interests, needs, and passions that constitutes the collective life of mankind. A linked criticism has been that liberalism lacks an adequate theory of power, failing to see the deep relationships between political phenomena and alignments of social class. (The theorist

*Occasionally, there are counterinstances suggesting that "vulgar Marxism" may meet with correction from within traditions it has debased. A leader of the Spanish Communist Party, one Luis, is quoted in *The New York Times* of October 29, 1975, saying: "We do not renounce a single one of the bourgeois liberties. If the bourgeoisie can dominate in freedom we want to provide more profound, more real liberties, not less. Socialism can provide the economic base for more complete liberty, without restricting a single aspect of bourgeois liberty." How much credence to give to this man's claim to democratic belief I do not know; but the fact that he speaks as he does must be regarded as significant.

Kenneth Minogue makes the point vividly: "The adjustment of interest conception [intrinsic to contemporary liberalism] . . . omits the crunch of truncheon on skull which always lies just in the background of political life. . . ."[2]) Still another linked criticism, in the line of Rousseau, proposes that modern man is torn apart by a conflict between the liberal acceptance of bourgeois institutions, which sanction the pursuit of selfish interest without regard to a larger community, and the liberal doctrine of popular sovereignty, which implies that the citizen must set aside private interests and concern himself with the common welfare.

Here, surely, it must be acknowledged that the socialist criticism—also made by nonsocialists—has all but completely conquered—indeed, become absorbed into—the thought even of those who oppose socialism and/or Marxism. Almost every sophisticated (and thereby, soon enough, unsophisticated) analysis of society now takes it for granted that politics must be closely related to, and more or less seen as a reflection of, social interest; that society forms a totality in which the various realms of activity, though separable analytically, are intertwined in reality; that no segment of the population can be assumed any longer to be mute or passive, and that there has appeared a major force, the working class, that must be taken into historical account; and that the rationalism of most liberal theory, though not (one hopes) simply to be dismissed, must be complicated by a recognition of motives and ends in social behavior that are much richer, more complicated, and deeply troubling.*

---

*A word about the role of the working class in socialist thought, as it contrasts with the frequent claims of liberalism to rise "above" mere class interest. Granted the common criticism that Marxism has over-

In our efforts both to understand history and to affect politics, there has occurred a "thickening" of our sense of society—indeed, the very idea of society, itself largely a nineteenth-century invention, testifies to that "thickening." We might even say that, as a result of Marx, there has occurred a "re-creation" of social reality. (The Christian historian Herbert Butterfield praises the Marxist approach to history in a vivid phrase, "it hugs the ground so closely"—which in his judgment does not prevent it from surveying what occurs in the upper reaches.) It is very hard, though some people manage, to see politics as a mere exercise for elites, or an unfolding of first principles; it is very hard to see politics apart from its relation to the interaction of classes, levels of productivity, modes of socioeconomic organization, etc. Writing in 1885 about his early work, Engels says:

---

estimated the revolutionary potential of the workers; granted that socialist rhetoric has sometimes romanticized the workers. It nevertheless remains that a major historical and moral conquest of the socialist movement, especially in the nineteenth century, was to enable the masses of the lowly—as liberalism only occasionally did, and with nothing like the same passion—to enter the stage of history and acquire a historical consciousness. Few developments in the last two centuries have so decisively helped the consolidation of democratic institutions; few have been so painfully exploited to violate democratic norms. It would be foolish to say that socialism alone should take credit for the entry of "the masses" into political life; but it was the socialists who gave this entry a distinct moral sanction. At its best, socialism enabled the formation of that impressive human type we know as the self-educated worker. That the rise of the working class to articulation and strength could, nevertheless, be exploited for authoritarian ends seems a major instance of the tragedy of progress.

> While I was in Manchester, it was tangibly brought home to me that the economic facts, which have so far played no role or only a contemptible one in the writing of history, are, at least in the modern world, a decisive historical force; that they form the basis of the origination of the present-day class antagonisms; that these class antagonisms, in the countries where they have become fully developed, thanks to large-scale industry, hence especially in England, are in their turn the basis of the formation of political parties and party struggles, and thus of all political history.[3]

If the germs of reductionism can be detected in such a passage, so too can the possibilities for complication and nuance: it all depends on which clause one chooses to stress. Anyone wishing to trace the development of modern social thought—among other things, from socialism to sociology—could do worse than start with a gloss on this passage from Engels.

The "economism," real or apparent, of the Engels passage was followed by a vulgarization in popular Marxist writings, but there is also present in the Marxist tradition another—and for our time crucial—view of the relation between state and society. In his earlier and middle years especially, Marx saw that the state could gain an autonomy of its own, rising "above" classes as a kind of smothering leviathan. (The state in Louis Napoleon's France, wrote Marx, was "an appalling parasitic body, which enmeshes the body of French society like a net and chokes all its pores."[4]) This perception could be crucial for a reconciliation between socialists and liberals—we shall come back to it.

Yet, from the vantage point of the late twentieth century, socialists ought to be self-critical enough to admit that the victory over liberalism with regard to such matters as the relationship between politics and society, state and economy, has by no means been an unambiguous one, certainly not a victory to bring unqualified satisfaction. Apart from reductionism, I would raise a point that seems increasingly important.

I have in mind what might be called the body of traditional political wisdom, or the reflections of thoughtful men on the "perennial" problems of politics. And to speak of "perennial" problems, I want to insist, is to locate them *within* a historical continuum.

In its historicist relativizing, its absorption with particular social circumstances, the socialist tradition has given rather short shrift to traditional political reflection. A pity: Marx might have been unsympathetic to Madison's reflections in *The Federalist* regarding the dynamics of faction in a republic; perhaps he would have seen them as excessively abstract or as a rationale for class interest. Yet both of these criticisms could be accepted without necessarily undermining the value of what Madison said. The socialist movement has suffered from its impatience with the accumulated insights of the centuries regarding political life. As a result, despite its prolonged attention to politics and its often brilliant analyses of political strategy, the socialist tradition has lacked, or refused, a theory of politics as an autonomous or at least distinct activity. It has had little to say, until recently, about such matters as necessary delimitations of power, the problems of representation, the uses or misuses of a division of authority, the relation between branches of government, etc.

A fascinating example: In late 1874 and early 1875 Marx read Bakunin's book *Statism and Anarchy,* made extended extracts, and attached to these his own, sharply polemical comments. Bakunin was anticipating one of the questions endlessly rehearsed by writers of the nonauthoritarian left—how to prevent the bureaucratization of a "workers' state," whether ex-workers raised to power would become corrupted, etc., etc. Bakunin writes:

> Universal suffrage—the right of the whole people—to elect its so-called representatives and rulers of the State—this is the last word of the Marxists as well as of the democratic school. And this is a falsehood behind which lurks the despotism of a governing minority. . . . But this minority, say the Marxists, will consist of workers. Yes, indeed, of *ex-workers, who, once they become rulers or representatives of the people, cease to be workers.*

At which point Marx interrupts: "No more than does a manufacturer today cease to be a capitalist on becoming a city councilman." Continues Bakunin: "From that time on they [the ex-workers] represent not the people but themselves and their own claims to govern the people. Those who doubt this know precious little about human nature."[5]

One need not acquiesce in Bakunin's hostility toward representative democratic institutions in order to see that, in his own way, he has hit upon one of the "perennial" problems in political thought—the problem of representation, how the elected representative of a group or class can become corrupted or bureaucratized upon acquiring power.

Marx's answer seems to me unsatisfactory: the manufacturer representing his class in a city council remains a manufacturer, retaining his commercial interests, whereas a worker elected to a city council ceases to be a worker and is thereby thrust into a new, problematic situation. The manager, though obviously susceptible to corruption, is not expected to help usher in a new, universal era—he need only defend particularistic interests—but the worker elected to office in a "workers' state" is burdened, according to the Marxist prescription, with great historical and moral responsibilities, which renders the problems of corruption and bureaucratism all the more acute. Surely Marx was able to understand this; but what made it hard for him to respond to such matters with sufficient seriousness was a historical method, an ideological bent, a political will.

Yet, hidden within the class analyses of the Marxists there have remained—a Marxist analysis of Marxism might suggest that there *must* remain—elements of traditional political thinking. Lenin, the one Marxist writer most impatient with talk about "perennial" problems, seems nevertheless to recognize in *State and Revolution* that a theory focusing upon change must also take into account continuity. He writes:

> Men . . . liberated from capitalist exploitation will gradually become accustomed to abide by the elementary rules of social life which have been known from time immemorial and have been set out for thousands of years in all regulations, and they will follow these rules without force, compulsion, subservience, and the special apparatus of compulsion which is known as the state.[6]

One wants to reply: But if there are "elementary rules of social life . . . known from time immemorial," rules that can be fully realized only in a classless society, then it must follow that in earlier, class-dominated societies those rules became manifest in some way; otherwise we could not recognize their existence. There are, then, "perennial" problems of politics, by no means so "elementary" either—considering the fact that they have never been entirely solved, nor seem likely ever to be entirely solved. And these problems cannot be dismissed by reference to class or historical contexts, though obviously class and historical contexts give them varying shape and significance. They are problems, it might be acknowledged, that have been discussed with greater depth by conservatives and liberals than by socialists.

The Marxist/socialist criticism of liberalism regarding the relation of politics to society now seems less cogent, or at least requires greater complication, than it did half a century ago. And this for an additional reason: with the growth of the modern industrial state, in both its Western and Eastern versions, politics takes on a new primacy—indeed, a kind of "independence"—vis-à-vis the institutions and mechanisms of the economy. In the communist countries what happens to the economy, what is done with one or another segment of the working class, how the peasants are treated in the kolkhoz: all stem from political decisions. Far from the ruling party bureaucracy's being a mere agency of, or even, as Trotsky believed, a parasite upon, one of the social classes, the party bureaucracy is the decisive sociopolitical force in the country, akin to a ruling class. State and society tend to merge in totalitarian countries, so that traditional discriminations between politics and economics come to seem of little use.

In advanced capitalist countries, the state increasingly takes over crucial functions of the market, while still allowing a considerable measure of autonomy to corporations and private business. These developments have been noted frequently; insofar as they persist, some of the apparently sealed conclusions from the long debate between liberalism and socialism need to be reopened. The traditional liberal notions of politics cannot simply be exhumed, but neither can the traditional socialist objections to them be repeated with confidence. What can be said, tentatively, is that the liberal insistence upon politics as a mode of autonomous human action with "laws" and "rules" of its own has come to have a new persuasiveness, not least of all within socialist thought.

There is a criticism of liberal politics and thought that runs through the whole of socialist literature but, by now, can also be heard at many points to the right and left of liberalism: among "organicist" conservatives, followers of the young Marx, Christian socialists, syndicalists, communitarian New Leftists. This criticism is most often expressed as a defense of the values of community—human fellowship, social grouping—against egotism, competition, private property. Necessarily, it raises questions about the quality of life in bourgeois society: the failure of a common culture, the heavy burdens placed upon the family when people lack alternative spheres of cooperative activity, the breakdown of social discipline that follows from laissez-faire. This criticism also takes a political form: the argument that democracy requires public life, that it cannot be successfully maintained in a society of privatized persons whose interests are confined to their families and businesses, and that public life depends upon a sharing of political and economic goods. The idea of economic man is declared to be a libel upon humanity; the vision of extreme individualism, an impoverishment of social possibility; and the kind of life likely to emerge from a society devoted to such ideas, a terrible drop from traditional humanist and Christian standards.

Most thoughtful liberals have by now acknowledged the force of this criticism. Indeed, there is rather little in it that cannot be found in John Stuart Mill's essays on Bentham and Coleridge. In the long run, then, freedom of criticism does seem to yield some benefits, does seem to prompt spokesmen for major political-intellectual outlooks to complicate and modify their thought. Liberal criticism has made a difference in socialism; socialist criticism, in liberalism.

Still, who does not feel the continued poignancy in the yearning for community, which seems so widespread in our time? Who does not respond, in our society, to the cry that life is poor in shared experiences, vital communities, free brother- and sister-hoods? Yet precisely the pertinence and power of this attack upon traditional liberalism must leave one somewhat uneasy. For we live in a time when the yearning for community has been mis-shaped into a gross denial of personal integrity, when the desire for the warmth of social bonds—marching together, living together, huddling together, complaining in concert—has helped to betray a portion of the world into the shame of the total state.

Let us be a little more cautious, then, in pressing the kind of attack upon liberalism that invokes an image of community—a little more cautious if only because this attack is so easy to press. There is indeed an element of the paltry in the more extreme versions of liberal individualism; but the alienation that has so frequently, and rightly, been deplored in recent decades may have its sources not just in the organization of society but in the condition of mankind. Perhaps it is even to be argued that there is something desirable in recognizing that, finally, nothing can fully protect us from the loneliness of ourselves.

A social animal, yes; but a solitary creature too. Socialists and liberals have some areas of common interest in balancing these two stresses, the communal and the individual, the shared and the alone. It is a balance that will tilt; men and women must be free to tilt it.*

---

*My friend Michael Walzer, reading a manuscript version of this essay, has made an observation that seems to me cogent at this point. I append it here (with his permission):

"You describe the communitarian critique of liberalism, acknowledge its power, but proceed quickly to note the distortions of communitarianism, and end by pleading for a balance between the communal and the individual. Stated this way, I don't disagree; but I think

---

Functioning for a good many decades as an opposition movement, and one, moreover, that could not quite decide whether it wished to be brought into society or preferred to seek a "total" revolutionary transformation, the socialist movement systematically attacked liberalism for timidity, evasiveness, vacillation, "rotten compromise," etc. It charged that liberalism was weak, that it never dared to challenge the socioeconomic power of the

---

that I would dwell longer than you do on the power of the critique and also try to argue that socialism is not the same as communitarianism —that it represents or might represent a kind of middle position between the solitary individual and the overheated community. I find myself increasingly uneasy about the triumph of liberal individualism. Consider: every new census shows more Americans living alone (in 'single-person households'); the divorce rate is now 50% for first marriages (considerably higher for second and third marriages) and rising; no-fault divorce has virtually ended child support payments, and as a result there has been a significant shift in social resources from children to single adults; rates of suicide, mental illness, alcoholism and drug addiction are all higher among adults living alone, etc., etc. All this is a result of liberal success; it's not the work of extremists, but of middle-of-the-road American state legislators and judges acting out of their conventional principles. I don't know what the alternative to liberal individualism is, but it's not, it doesn't have to be, a Rousseauian communitarianism; it might have more to do with such old socialist values as cooperation, mutuality, communal provision, public life, and so on. The truth is that life in a liberal society has been made bearable by the existence of social ties that liberalism does not create and apparently does not sustain, and one of the things that socialism is or ought to be about is the creation of new ties (and sometimes the strengthening of old ones)."

bourgeoisie, that it was mired in what Trotsky called "parliamentary cretinism," etc.

The historical impact of this criticism can hardly be overestimated. A major source of the "welfare state" has surely been the pressure that socialist movements have exerted upon a liberalism that has long moved past its early élan. Insofar as the socialist criticism served to force liberalism to a militant posture in coping with social injustice, the results have been for the better.

But also—for the worse. For the socialist criticism (as the rise of Bolshevism and its various offshoots make clear) contained at least two strands: one that disdained liberalism for its failure to live up to its claims, and one that disdained liberalism for its success in living up to its claims. We touch here upon a great intellectual scandal of the age: the tacit collaboration of right and left extremes in undermining the social and moral foundations of liberalism. In the decades between the Paris Commune and World War II both right- and left-wing intellectuals were gravely mistaken, and morally culpable, in their easy and contemptuous dismissal of liberalism. That the society they saw as the embodiment of bourgeois liberalism required scathing criticism I do not doubt. But they failed utterly to estimate the limits of what was historically possible in their time, as they failed, even more important, to consider what the consequences might be of their intemperate attacks upon liberalism. It was all very well to denounce liberalism as what Ezra Pound called—Lenin would have agreed—"a mess of mush," but to assault the vulnerable foundations of liberal democracy meant to bring into play social forces the intellectuals of both right and left could not foresee. There were, as it turned out, far worse things in the world than "a mess of mush."

Bourgeois Europe was overripe for social change by the time

of World War I. But the assumptions that such change required a trampling on liberal values in the name of hierarchical order or proletarian dictatorship, and that liberal values were inseparable from cultural decadence and capitalist economy—these assumptions proved a disaster. In the joyful brutality of their verbal violence many intellectuals, at both ends of the political spectrum, did not realize how profound a stake they had in preserving the norms of liberalism. They felt free to sneer at liberalism because, in a sense, they remained within its psychological orbit; they could not really imagine its destruction and took for granted that they would continue to enjoy its shelter. Even the most authoritarian among them could not foresee a situation in which *their* freedom would be destroyed. Dreaming of natural aristocrats or sublime proletarians, they helped pave the way for maniac lumpen.

Still another socialist/radical criticism of liberalism, familiar from polemics of the 1930s but urgently revived during the 1960s by the New Left, is that the structure of liberties in democratic society rests on a shared acquiescence in the continued power of the bourgeoisie; that these liberties survive on condition they not be put to the crucial test of basic social transformation; and that they might well be destroyed by the bourgeoisie or its military agencies if a serious effort were made by a democratically elected government to introduce socialist economic measures. The overthrow of the Allende regime in Chile has been cited as a telling confirmation.

It is an old problem. Marx and Engels suggested that a socialist transition in such countries as England and Holland, with their deep-rooted democratic traditions, might be peaceful. Most other European countries not yet having completed the "bourgeois revolution" by the mid-nineteenth century, it seemed reasonable to the founders of "scientific socialism" that revolutionary methods might be necessary on the Continent—though we also know that later, when the German social democracy became a mass party, Engels accepted the parliamentary course. The standard Bolshevik gloss would be that since the time Marx and Engels had written, the bourgeois state in England and Holland had grown more powerful, developing a traditional apparatus of repression, and that the expectation of peaceful transition had therefore become obsolete.

I think it would be an error to dismiss the Marxist criticism on this point as merely outmoded or irrelevant. Changes in class rule have in the past rarely come about without one or another quantity of violence, and, as I remember hearing and saying in my youth, ruling classes don't just fold up their tents and slink away. By the same token, I now reply to my younger self, past changes in class rule have rarely, if ever, taken place within established democratic societies, hence could not be said to provide a test of the socioeconomic strains democratic societies can be expected to sustain.

To insist that liberalism and/or liberties must collapse under a serious effort to introduce socialist measures signifies (a) an unfortunate concession to those right-wing ideologues who insist that political liberty is inseparable from and could not survive the destruction of private property, or (b) a vision of socialist transformation so apocalyptic and "total" that the collapse of political liberties in such circumstances might as readily be the work of revolutionary insurgents as of a resistant bourgeoisie.

As for the historical evidence, it seems mixed. A very great deal depends on the strength of attachment among a people to democratic values; only a bit less, on the ability of a given society to avoid the kind of economic cataclysms that would put this attachment under excessive strain. If, say, European social-democratic governments, ruling with substantial majorities and elected as parties pledged to go considerably beyond welfare-state measures, were to introduce extensive socialist proposals, there is not much reason to expect major extralegal efforts to undo their policies.* For the tradition of pacific social life and "playing by the rules" seems strong enough in such countries for them to envisage a major onslaught against the power of corporations and large businesses without risking the survival of democracy. (I referred a few sentences back to governments with substantial majorities. It seems reasonable, after all, that a government squeaking into office with a narrow margin should exercise restraints in introducing major social change.)

It is by no means clear that the Chilean experience "proves" that a democratic path to socialism is impossible. What it may prove is (a) that a left-wing government trying to maintain democratic norms while introducing major social change must be especially sensitive to the interests and sentiments of the middle class; and (b) that the army, acting out of its own interests and sentiments, can become an independent political force, establishing a dictatorial regime that it would be a mistake to see as a mere creature of bourgeois restoration.

---

*Harold Laski, in his *Parliamentary Government in England* (London, 1938), questioned whether democracy could survive if a Labour government came to power and legislated a socialist program. In 1945, a Labour government did come to power and legislated, if not a socialist program, then a huge welfare-state program decidedly akin, or at least pointing the way, to socialism. And democracy did not collapse. This does not yet "prove" that Laski was wrong, only that it would be unwise to assume that he was right.

The role of armies in contemporary politics is a fascinating problem, beyond discussion here, except for this: in a variety of circumstances, but especially where a mutual weakening of antagonistic classes has occurred, the army (like the state) can take on unexpected strength and autonomy. Nor is it clear that this follows the traditional Marxist expectation that the army would be employed by the ruling class to save its endangered interests. Even if that was true in Chile, it has not been true in either Portugal or Greece. In Asian and African countries, the role of the army is evidently that of a makeshift power compensating for the feebleness of all social classes. There is, then, something new here, not quite anticipated in liberal or socialist thought.

The question whether a liberal-democratic regime can peacefully sustain major social or socialist changes remains open. If a categorical negative is unwarranted, so too is an easy reassurance. Given the probable configuration of politics in the Western democracies, there is some reason to conclude that even left-socialist regimes staying within democratic limits would have to proceed more cautiously, with greater respect for the multiplicity of group interests, than the usual leftist expectations have allowed. And the anxiety provoked by a possible effort to combine liberal polity with socialist economy remains a genuine anxiety, shared by both liberals and socialists.

If we confine ourselves to the "advanced" countries, one criticism socialists have come increasingly to make of liberalism is that it fails to extend sufficiently its democratic concerns from the political to the economic realm.* Early in the century, the distin-

*A criticism anticipated in general terms by the early Marx: "Political emancipation is indeed a great step forward. It is not, to be sure, the final form of universal human emancipation, but is the final form *within*

guished British liberal writer L. T. Hobhouse put the matter elegantly: "Liberty without equality is a name of noble sound and squalid result." I will not linger on this point except to make the following observations:

It suggests that the difference between social liberalism and democratic socialism keeps growing smaller, so that at some point that difference may become no more than incremental. Both traditional liberal thinkers and Marxist theoreticians would deny this; a good many social democrats, in effect, believe it.

It leaves aside what in a fuller consideration could not be left aside: that there remain serious liberal criticisms of socialist proposals, such as that efforts to legislate greater equality of wealth, income, and power in economic life could seriously impair political liberty, and that the statist version of socialism (the only realistic one, say some liberal critics) would bring about a fearful concentration of power.

We may be ready to subscribe to the socialist criticism that modern liberalism fails sufficiently to extend its democratic concerns to economic life—for example, the governance of corporations; we may also share the socialist desire for greater participation of the masses in political and economic decision-making; but, to turn things around, I would take quite seriously the liberal skepticism about schemes involving "mass" or "direct" democ-

---

the prevailing order of things. . . . Where the political state has achieved its full development, man leads a double life, a heavenly and an earthly life, not only in thought or consciousness but in *actuality*. In the *political community* he regards himself as a *communal being*; but in *civil society* he is active as a *private individual,* treats other men as means, reduces himself to a means, and becomes the plaything of alien powers."

racy. Such schemes, insofar as they would brush aside representative institutions (elections, parliaments, etc.) in favor of some sort (but which sort?) of "direct" or "participatory" rule, are likely to end up as hopelessly vague or as prey to demagogic techniques for manipulating those who "participate" in movements, meetings, plebiscites, etc. If the survival of democracy depends on greater popular participation, greater popular participation by no means ensures or necessarily entails the survival of democracy. Under modern conditions, representative institutions are indispensable to democratic societies; any proposals for "transcending" them, even if they come through socialist good will, should be regarded with suspicion.

There is, finally, the plenitude of attacks directed against liberalism along a spectrum of positions ranging from the reactionary to the revolutionary, most of them chastising its "deeper" failures as a philosophical outlook.

Liberalism, we are told, accepts an egalitarianism that a day or two spent with open eyes in our mass society shows to be insupportable—while Professor Leo Strauss makes clear the traditional warrants and esoteric virtues of hierarchy. Liberalism proposes a belief in rational harmony, the "illusion" (to quote Kenneth Minogue) "of ultimate agreement" among men, "and perhaps most central of all, the ideal that will and desire can ultimately be sovereign in human affairs"[7]—while Professor Michael Oakeshott tells us that life is muddle, that efforts at rational structuring of our affairs are likely to lead to still greater muddle, even, perhaps, to tyranny. Liberalism congeals into the simplistic notion, as Lionel Trilling has written, "that the life of man can be nicely settled by correct social organization, or short of that, by the election of high moral attitudes." Liberalism, focusing obsessively upon change, distracts us from the essentials of existence largely beyond the grasp of mere reason or public agency. Liberalism has a false view of the human situation, refusing to take into account the irrationalities and aggressions of our nature. (How can a liberal cope with the realities of the Hobbesian jungle? What can a goodhearted liberal make of the Freudian view of the human heart?) Liberalism ignores or dispatches the tragic sense of life, turning people away from the suffering that is unavoidable (perhaps even good?) in our experience. Liberalism replaces the warming cohesion of traditional communities with a rootless anonymity. Liberalism cannot cope with the mysteries of death, as Christianity does through its myth of resurrection, or existentialism tries to do through its unblinking gaze into the void.

What is one to say of these criticisms? That often they confuse the historical genesis of liberalism, accompanied as it was by excessive claims, with later and more realistic versions of liberalism; that the alleged rootlessness of liberal man, though clearly surrounded with difficulties, also has brought unprecedented freedoms and opportunities—indeed, entire new visions of the self; that the increasing stress of modern liberal thought upon a pluralist society indicates at least some recognition of clashing interests, irreconcilable needs, confrontations of class; that a recognition of the irrational and aggressive components of human conduct can become an argument in favor of limitations upon power favored by liberalism; that we may recognize weaknesses and limitations in liberalism as a *Weltanschauung*—indeed, refuse to see it as a *Weltanschauung*—while still fervently believing that a liberal polity allows for the best realization of human diversity and freedom; and that there is no necessary conflict between "dark" views of the human condition and an acceptance of the liberal style in public life.

Let us grant, then, some of the criticisms made of liberal afflatus (usually in the far past) and liberal smugness (usually in the recent past) and admit, as well, the probability that insofar as men need religious myths and rites to get through their time on earth, liberalism is not likely to offer satisfaction. What must be stressed, all the same, is that a commitment to the liberal style in politics does not necessarily imply a commitment to a total world-view claiming to include all experience, from private fantasy to public authority. (Perhaps we would all be better off, for a time, without total world-views.)

Toward these and similar exchanges between liberalism and its critics, socialists have shown a very wide range of responses. The more extreme leftist tendencies, verging on the authoritarian and chiliastic, have been tempted to borrow some of the arguments of the right, especially those releasing contempt for the flaccid moderation of liberalism, its alleged failures to confront painful realities of social life and human nature. But for those socialists who largely accept the premises of a liberal polity, there are other problems, notably the disconcerting fact that the bulk of the philosophical-existential criticism directed against liberalism can be brought to bear with equal cogency against social democracy.

3.

Unavoidably this leads to the question: Apart from whatever capacity both liberalism and social democracy show for handling our socioeconomic difficulties, how well can they cope with—I choose deliberately a portentous term—the crisis of civilization that many people feel to be encompassing our lives? The crisis of civilization that besets the twentieth century has to do, in part, with a breakdown in the transmission and common acceptance of values—which may also be a way of saying, with residual but powerful yearnings toward transcendence. Insofar as this occurs, there follows a pervasive uncertainty as to the "meanings" and ends of existence. One sign of this crisis is a resurgence of strident contempt for the ethic of liberal discourse and the style of rationality. Partly this arises from the mixed failings and successes of the welfare state, but partly from an upswell of ill-understood religious sentiments that are unable to find a proper religious outlet and become twisted into moral-political absolutism, a hunger for total solutions and apocalyptic visions.

The customary rationalism of earlier generations of socialists (and liberals too) could hardly grasp such a development. Yet, no matter how distant we may be from the religious outlook, we must ask ourselves whether the trouble of our time isn't partly a consequence of that despairing emptiness which has followed the breakup of traditional religious systems in the nineteenth century; whether the nihilism that sensitive people feel to be seeping through their lives may not itself testify to a kind of inverted religious aspiration; whether the sense of moral disorientation that often afflicts us isn't due to the difficulties of keeping alive a high civilization without a sustaining structure of belief.

Perhaps, in honesty, there really is no choice but to live with the uncomfortable aftereffects of the disintegration of religious belief, which has brought not only the positive consequences some of us hoped for but also others that leave us discomfited. In any case, nothing seems more dubious than the impulse I detect these days among some rightward-moving intellectuals: a willing of faith in behalf of alleged social-moral benefits. Here, finally, liberals and democratic socialists find themselves in the same boat, even if at opposite ends of it. The Fabian course to which some of us are committed seems to me politically good and perhaps even realistic, but we ought to acknowledge that this course fails to stir the passions of many people. We ought to acknowledge that between the politics we see as necessary and the expressive-emotional needs that break out recurrently in Western society there are likely to be notable gaps. We can only worry about this matter, recognizing that it may be one of those instances where virtue entails formidable deficits.

But let me end on a somewhat more hopeful note. Half a century from now, one fact about our time may come to be seen as the most crucial. Whatever the separate or linked failures of liberalism and democratic socialism may be, there have come to us these past few decades voices from the East superbly reasserting the values of freedom, tolerance, and openness of discourse. These men and women have, thus far, "failed"; they have been destroyed, imprisoned, humiliated, isolated. Yet their very appearance signifies an enormous moral triumph for liberalism and, perhaps, democratic socialism. Beneath the snow, the seed has lived.

Thinking about Socialism

Christianity did not "die" in the nineteenth century. Millions held fast to the faith; churches survived; theological controversies flourished. Yet we can now see that in the decades after the Enlightenment, Christianity suffered deep wounds, which could not be healed—sometimes were even made worse—by the sincere efforts of various thinkers to refine and revise the faith. Gradually Christianity lost its claim to speak for the whole of Western culture; gradually it lost the ability to seize and hold the imagination of serious young people. Some of them it could still attract, but not with the assurance of the past.

Has something like this been happening to socialism these past several decades? Powerful parties in Europe still employ the socialist vocabulary, and millions of people still accept the socialist label, yet some deep inner crisis of belief, to say nothing of public failures and defeats, has beset socialism. The soaring passions of the early movement are gone, and those of us who strive for socialist renewal cannot help wondering whether we are caught in a drift of historical decline, perhaps beyond reversing, perhaps to yield at some future moment to a new radical humanism. And perhaps too it does not really matter: each generation must do what it can.

"To the question of the elements of social restructure [i.e., socialism] Marx and Engels never gave a positive answer, because they had no inner relation to the idea. Marx might occasionally allude to 'the elements of the new society' . . . but the political act of revolution remained the one thing worth striving for."[1]

This observation by Martin Buber, while slightly overstated, embodies an essential truth. Marx and Engels praised the early-nineteenth-century "utopian socialists" for their boldness in projecting visions of a new Golden Age, but they were also contemptuous of the utopians' habit of indulging in detailed "future-painting." Whereas the utopians, wrote Marx, pictured a socialist society as "an ideal to which reality will have to adjust itself,"[2] he saw the movement toward socialism as a necessary outcome of concrete social conflicts. He wanted to place the socialist project within the course of historical development, and this he did by specifying two driving forces within history: first, the evolution of economic techniques and structures, leading to a concentration of ownership and wealth, a recurrence of social crisis, and a sharpening of class conflict; and second, the gathering strength and rising consciousness of the working class, derived from or enabled by its crucial position within capitalist economy. By now it seems clear that Marx was keener in analyzing the "driving forces" of the economy than in allocating the "tasks" of the proletariat, a class that has shown itself capable of intermittent rebellion but not, at least thus far, of serving as the pivot of socialist transformation.

To read the passages in Marx's writings that deal with the socialist future—they are scattered, infrequent, and fragmentary—is to recognize how valid is the charge that on this matter he slips into a vague and static perfectionism. What we get from his remarks is a vision of a world marvelously free of social—and, indeed, nonsocial—conflict: no longer in thrall to alienation, exploitation, and social fetishism, humanity reaches, for the first time, a high plateau of the human. In the Marxist anticipation of the good society there is little recognition of the sheer recalcitrance of all social arrangements, the limitations that characterize the human species, the likely persistence into the future of error, stupidity, and ill-will. Even convinced socialists must by now feel some skepticism about this version of utopia, free of conflicts, free of mundane problems.

Marxists would reply, with some irritation, that their vision of ultimate social harmony depends on the unfolding of a lengthy historical sequence during which not just new values and habits but a new humanity would emerge. Perhaps so. There is no way to disprove such expectations, any more than to dispel the skepticism they arouse. Far more troubling, at least for a socialist living toward the end of the twentieth century, is the fact that this vision of a society in which "the state withers away" and "the antithesis between physical and mental labor vanishes" does very little to help us achieve a qualitatively better, if still imperfect, society—the kind that some of us call socialism.

Yet it's only fair to add that Marx's failure to engage critically with the problem of the envisaged socialist society did have some positive aspects. If the society of the future is to be entrusted to its living actors, then Marx was right, perhaps, in thinking it imprudent to detail its features in advance. History must be left to those who will make it.

But there is another, less attractive reason for Marx's failure to draw "the face" of a socialist society. Marxism offers a strong theory of social change but has little to say about political arrangements—structures of government, balances of power, agencies of representation. Marxism has usually failed to consider with sufficient attention what we might call the trans- or supraclass elements of politics—those elements likely to be present (and perplexing) in any society. Except for some brilliant remarks in *The Eighteenth Brumaire of Louis Bonaparte,* Marx gave little weight to politics as an autonomous activity, politics as more than epiphenomenon, politics as a realm with its own powers, procedures, and norms. As Paul Ricoeur has written, "Politics embodies a human relationship which is not reducible to class conflict or socioeconomic tensions. . . . Even the state most in subjection to a dominant class is also a state precisely to the extent that it expresses the fundamental will of the nation as a whole. . . . On the other hand, politics develops evils of its own —evils specific to the exercise of power."[3]

From such perceptions there follows a problematic view of the entire process of change that is supposed to lead to socialism. But if some sophisticated Marxists have recently begun to recognize the autonomy of politics, it must in honesty be added that this was by no means the prevalent view of the socialist movement during its formative, most powerful years. During the three or four decades after Marx's death, the movement as an institution grew stronger, but its vision of the goal for which it was striving declined into a slackness of perfection, only tenuously, through a papery chain of rhetoric, related to the issues and struggles of the moment. Socialism came gradually to be "defined" as a condition of classlessness, the possibility and nature of which were seen more as premise than problem; and since the inclination of Marxists was to think about conflicts and evils as the consequence of class domination, it followed—did it not?—that the eradication of classes must sooner or later mean the disappearance of these afflictions. I exaggerate a little, but not, I fear, by very much.

Among social democrats this habit of thought encouraged an easy confidence in the benefits of historical evolution; among revolutionary Marxists, a faith in the self-elected vanguard party that would satisfy the ends of history.

Until about World War I, this genial mythicizing of an assured future may not have done too much damage, for in those early years the main work of the left was to rouse the previously mute lower classes to the need for historical action. Indeed, the visionary tone of early Marxism helped give the workers a quasi-religious confidence in their own powers. Had the movement achieved nothing else, this arousal of the plebes would still be to its credit. In fact, it also helped bring about valuable social changes, a sequence of reforms eventuating in the welfare state.

The problem of socialism would become acute when a socialist movement approached power, or in quite different circumstances, when it was weak and under sharp intellectual attack. In both of these extreme circumstances, the poverty of Marxist (not all socialist) thought regarding the "face of socialism" becomes very serious. Between immediate struggles for specific reforms and rosy invocations of the cooperative commonwealth still to come, *a whole space is missing*—the space of social reconstruction. In the writings of the English guild socialists we find some hints on these matters, but not enough. Only in the last fifteen or twenty years, under the impact of crisis and defeat, has some of that "missing space" been occupied through the writings of a number of serious thinkers—I shall be discussing them later—who have tried to offer some guidelines (not blueprints) for a socialist society. The work is just beginning. Can it still be in time? I do not know.

2.

Why has the European social democracy been unable to advance further than the welfare state of Scandinavia? I list some of the possible answers: Social-democratic parties often came to office without parliamentary majorities, which meant they had to enter coalitions that imposed severe constraints. Social-democratic parties were often voted into office at moments when capitalist economies were suffering breakdowns, which meant that precisely the condition prompting their victories also limited their capacity for taking radical measures. Social-democratic parties in office frequently had to face flights of capital, a problem that, within the limits of the nation-state, proved very difficult to cope with. And social-democratic parties, settling into the routines of institutional life, began to lose their radical edge.

For my present purposes, however, I want to stress another, important if not decisive reason for the difficulties of social-democratic parties. They often had no clear idea, no worked-out vision, of what a socialist transformation might entail. Given their commitment to democracy, their justified distaste for Bolshevik dictatorship, and their recognition that a good part of their electorate cared more about particular measures than a new society, they began to find the idea of socialism increasingly slippery, evanescent, insubstantial. No doubt, in some instances there were also the betrayals of principle that the far left charged against social democracy, but most of the time, I think, it was victimized by its own intellectual slackness. The social democrats thought they knew what had to be done the next day, but when it came to their sacred "historic mission" they often grew uncertain and timid. And sometimes they were struck dumb.

Not so the Bolsheviks. *They knew.* Their aura of certainty, their persuasion that history lay snugly in the party's fist, helped the communists win the support of many European workers and intellectuals during the years between world wars. Yet even a glance at the Bolshevik record after the November 1917 revolution will show that Lenin and his comrades had only the most sketchy and confused ideas about the socioeconomic policies that might enable a socialist transformation. The seizure of power—about *that* they could speak with authority.

Shortly before the Russian Revolution, Lenin had written that if the Bolsheviks came to power in backward, war-devastated Russia, they would establish "workers' control" over industry; but he did not propose large-scale nationalizations. From November 1917 to the summer of 1918, the Bolsheviks favored what we'd now call a mixed economy, in which, for a time at least, large areas of private ownership of industry would continue, but production and investment decisions would be controlled by the leftist state together, presumably, with working-class institutions. This view was in accord with Lenin's realistic understanding that socialism—seen traditionally by Marxists as a society presupposing economic abundance and a high level of culture—could not be achieved in a country like Russia, certainly not without substantial aid from the industrial West.

Once in power, the Bolsheviks veered wildly in their economic policies. At the start of the civil war they abandoned their initial moderation and introduced the draconian measures of war communism: virtually complete nationalization of enterprises, the requisitioning of agricultural products, and a highly centralized political-economic command. Many Bolsheviks came to regard all this as the appropriate road to socialism, though in later years some of them would admit that grave errors had been made, with the necessities of an extreme situation being mistakenly elevated into general principles.

War communism intensified the economic disaster that was already well advanced as a result of Russian defeat in the war. There now followed a sharp drop in production; further depletion of industrial plant; a radical cut in the size of the working class; a decline in labor productivity, etc. Some of these setbacks were a result of difficulties created by the civil war; some due to a mixture of Bolshevik arrogance and inexperience; but some the fruit of a by-now-habitual refusal on the left to think concretely, problematically, about the social transformation that might follow the assumption of political power.

Between 1917 and 1923, Bolshevik oscillations on economic policy found a vivid reflection in Trotsky's writings. At one point he proposed the creation of labor armies, a kind of militarized garrison economy; this ghastly idea, meeting with bitter resistance from Bolshevik and other trade unionists, was rejected. At another point, veering sharply, Trotsky proposed an economic course anticipating the New Economic Policy that would in fact be introduced in 1921: a considerable loosening of state controls, a return to a partly free market, something like a mixed economy. This proposal was at first rejected by the Bolsheviks, but under the pressures of reality they finally introduced the NEP. What we can see here is a deep incoherence, a floundering by gifted ideologues who had not anticipated, while still out of power and in a position to think theoretically, that the taking of power would by no means exempt them from the difficulties faced by their adversaries.

In his biography of the "right" Bolshevik leader Bukharin, Stephen F. Cohen remarks that Lenin took a "censorious attitude toward discussing future problems. He preferred Napoleon's advice, 'On s'engage et puis . . . on voit.'"[4] "One engages, and then one sees." Alas, we have seen.

3.

Were I writing a comprehensive study of modern socialism, a central emphasis would have to be put on the enormous damage wrought by Stalinism once it grew powerful in the 1930s. Insofar as right- and left-wing dogmatists found it convenient to identify the Russian dictatorship with socialism, they joined to discredit the entire socialist idea. And insofar as that identification grew popular, so too did the discrediting.

One result was that the already festering crisis of socialist thought became more severe. For the past several decades the socialist experience has involved a dislodgment of received persuasions, a melting-down of ideological structures, and a search for new—or for cleansed and reaffirmed old—values. For the socialists themselves this has often been a clarifying and chastening experience; but for their movement it brought grave difficulties. Introspection rarely makes for public effectiveness.

Many socialists of my generation would customarily defend their beliefs through what I'd call a hygienic negative: "We entirely reject any sort of party-state dictatorship: the very thought of it is appalling. Nor do we want a complete nationalization of industry. . . . Less and less does that seem an avenue to the cooperative commonwealth."

After a time such responses came close to being instinctive. Serious socialists would now describe the desired society by invoking desired *qualities,* with a stress on sentiments of freedom, attitudes of fraternity, and, sometimes, priorities of social allocation. They proposed, first of all, to secure the socialist idea in the realm of values, whereas, to simplify a little, the tradition in which some of us had been raised was one that focused on institutional changes. In making this shift, these socialists were doing something morally and politically necessary, but also tactically disabling. For unless plausible social structures and agencies could be located for realizing the values that were now being placed at the center of socialist thought, we were finally left with little more than our good will.*

---

*An illuminating parallel can be found in a passage from the British philosopher Stuart Hampshire: "For me socialism is not so much a theory as a set of moral injunctions, which seem to me clearly right and rationally justifiable: first, that the elimination of poverty ought to be the first priority of government after defense; secondly, that as great inequalities in wealth between different social groups lead to inequalities in power and in freedom of action, they are generally unjust and need to be redressed by governmental action; thirdly, that democratically elected governments ought to ensure that primary and basic human needs are given priority within the economic system, even if this involves some loss in the aggregate of goods and services which would otherwise be available. How these moral requirements are best realized, at particular times and places . . . are matters for the social sciences and also for a critical reading of history; after them also for personal experience and for worldly insight. . . ."[5]

Now I find this very sympathetic, but suspect it's open to the charge that it contains nothing distinctively socialist. Could not many liberals endorse Stuart Hampshire's "moral injunctions"? It's only when we come to specific proposals for putting these injunctions into practice that the socialist case can be said to stand or fall.

Nevertheless, the clarification of socialist values was the essential task during, say, the past half century: little of importance could be accomplished on the left until that was done. And if these values are now accepted as truisms, it is because a bitter struggle had to be conducted in their behalf. It is useful to restate a few:

- There is no necessary historical sequence from capitalism to socialism, or any irrefutable reason for supposing history moves along a steadily upward curve. Unforeseen societies—mixed, retrogressive, opaque—can persist for long periods of time.

- The abolition of capitalism is not necessarily a step toward human liberation; it can lead, and has led, to societies far more repressive than capitalism at its worst.

- Socialism is not to be "defined" as a society in which private property has been abolished; what is decisive is the political character of the regime exercising control over a postcapitalist or mixed economy.

- A "complete" transformation of humanity is a corrupt fantasy that can lead to a mixture of terror and apathy.

- Socialism should be envisaged as a society in which the means of production, to an extent that need not be rigidly determined in advance, are collectively or socially owned—which means democratically controlled. An absolute prerequisite is the preservation and growth of democracy.

One painful yet predictable result of this reshaping, or cleansed reassertion, of the socialist idea was that in the very course of acquiring an increasingly humane and democratic character, it also came to suffer from greater uncertainty with regard to social arrangements and institutional mechanisms. The reassertion of values led to skepticism about certain elements of traditional Marxist thought. Three instances:

1. *The assumption that the proletariat would serve as the leading agency of social transformation.*

History has vetoed this idea. The working class has not been able to "transcend" its role within capitalist society, except perhaps during brief outbursts of rebellion; and now, as a result of technological innovations, its specific gravity as social class and political actor seems to be in decline.* As if in response to this development, there has appeared a tendency to regard socialism as a goal transcending the interests of one or another class. There is something attractive about this, but also something that betrays political uncertainty. For to say that a social vision is the province of all, risks making it the passion of none.

2. *The assumption that the nationalization of industry would, if accompanied by a socialist winning of office, smooth the way for the new society.*

Significant socialist texts can readily be cited that make it clear that nationalization is not necessarily to be taken as an equivalent or even a precondition of socialism.† Yet it would be misleading

---

*As a matter of historical justice, I should add that if once we free the working class from the "tasks" imposed on it by Marxism, we can recognize that, as the main unpropertied class in modern society, it has exerted a strong and positive pressure to bring about major improvements in the social order.

†As far back as 1892, Karl Kautsky, an accredited legatee of Marx, wrote: "It does not follow that every nationalization of an economic function or an industry is a step toward the cooperative common-

to lean too heavily on these texts, since I am certain that an appeal to older socialists would yield the recollection that in the movement there has been a strong habitual tendency to put great faith in the value of nationalization.

In the communist dictatorships the mere takeover of industry has made for a frightful concentration (and fusion) of political and economic power. In some capitalist countries, portions of the economy have been nationalized, sometimes because socialist governments wished to make at least a dent in bourgeois ownership, sometimes because governments, bourgeois or socialist, came to the rescue of enterprises on the rim of bankruptcy. The results have not been very inspiring, especially when no efforts were made to introduce democratic participation by workers in the management of the newly nationalized industries.

Serious problems have arisen in the operation of such industries, some of them due to the inherent difficulties of functioning by a calculus of profit while trying, within an economy still largely capitalist, to satisfy social goals. What should be the

---

wealth. . . . If the modern state nationalizes certain industries, it does not do so for the purpose of restricting capitalist exploitation, but for the purpose of protecting the capitalist system. . . . As an exploiter of labor, the state is superior to any private capitalist."[6]

And Morris Hillquit, the American socialist leader: "Socialists entertain no illusions as to the benefits of governmentally-owned industries under the present regime. . . . Its effect may be decidedly reactionary. . . . The demand for national or municipal ownership of industries is always qualified [by socialists] with a provision for the democratic administration of such industries. . . ."[7]

I cite these two influential figures to show that such ideas do go back to earlier generations of socialist thinkers.

criteria for measuring efficiency in nationalized enterprises? If they are taken over because they have failed in private hands, what order of losses should society be prepared to accept? How are decisions to be made regarding capital investment? Such questions can be answered; and in part the answers are similar to those that might be provided with regard to private enterprise (since the criterion of profitability cannot simply be dismissed); but the answers should also be different from those prevailing under private enterprise (since such factors as "externalities" are now to be taken into systematic account).

Nationalization of industry has been part of a world-wide drift toward the interpenetration of state and society. It can be a device for trying to solve a crisis of capitalist economy; it can perhaps help to create a modern infrastructure in third-world economies; it can form part of the breakdown of "civil society" that enables the rise of totalitarianism; and it can be initiated by a socialist government intent upon deepening democratic practices in all areas of social life. Nationalization seems, in short, to be a somewhat neutral device, available to just about every kind of government: but whatever else, it is surely not a sufficient condition for a socialist transformation.

3. *The assumption that economic planning is a unique aspect or virtue of socialist society, ensuring both justice and orderliness in economic affairs, such as unplanned economies are not likely to match.*

By now we have learned otherwise. Planning does not necessarily offer an encompassing method for the solution of socioeconomic problems. As earlier Marxists like Kautsky and Bukharin glimpsed, planning does not have to wait for the happy arrival of socialism, but is at least partly to be found in "late"—that is, monopoly or cartel—versions of capitalism. Like any other human enterprise, planning is subject to error, manipulation, bureaucratic sluggishness, and sheer ill-will, so that it must always be tentative, proximate, and fallible. "Total" planning—that is, a command economy—entails authoritarian political structures. Democratic planning, upon which some socialists place great hopes, is at once attractive, complex, and problematic. There are ways in which planning must always be somewhat at odds with democratic procedures, if only because it often depends, in modern societies, on skilled professionals likely to develop their own caste or bureaucratic interests. On the other hand, "popular participation [can] inform the planner about the social terrain he is trying to map; the planner [can] facilitate the democratic process by presenting to the people intelligent alternatives for their choice."[8] No assertion of general principles or intent can remove the constant need for a nuanced and vigilant mediation between agencies of planning and a political democracy.

If, then, one considers the revisions in socialist thinking that we have had to make in recent decades, it becomes clear that we find ourselves in an uncomfortable but, I would contend, worthwhile difficulty—refining our values, growing somewhat uncertain about our means, sloughing off old ideological baggage. Leszek Kolakowski puts this matter well:

> Where are we now? What we lack in our thinking about society in socialist terms is not general values . . . but rather knowledge about how these values can be prevented from clashing with each other when put into practice. . . .
>
> Are we [then] fools to keep thinking in socialist terms? I do not think so. Whatever has been done in Western Europe to bring about more justice, more security, more educational opportunities, more welfare . . . could never have been achieved without the pressures of socialist ideologies and movements, for all

> their naïvetés and illusions. This does not mean that we are exculpated in advance and allowed to cherish these illusions endlessly, after so many defeats.[9]

During the last fifteen or twenty years, then, we have seen a significant shift in the nature and direction of socialist thought. The clarification of values toward which some of us had to devote major energies has now been achieved, at least in part, and as a result socialist thinkers have been able to turn to a study of those institutions and mechanisms through which these values might be realized in actuality.

4.

A number of writers have tackled the problems that seem likely to appear during a "transition period" between capitalism and socialism. Writers like Alec Nove, Michael Harrington, and Radoslav Selucky have offered proposals for the kind of immediate reforms (civil rights, women's rights, racial equality) that are not uniquely socialist in character but upon which liberals and socialists can happily agree. Next would come "structural reforms," such as tax proposals aiming at a gradual redistribution of income and wealth, and efforts to achieve full employment, which would surely entail some overall economic planning. These latter "structural reforms" might be described as extending and deepening the welfare state. Beyond this second group of proposals lies a third—those that would begin to change the fundamental relationships of power and property, such as a "challenge to corporate control of the investment process by insisting that public policy concern itself with what is produced . . . [to] include public controls over private investment decisions, such as specifying the conditions under which corporations can leave a locality or oligopolies can raise prices. . . ."[10] Steps might also be taken toward creating "social property," pilot projects of enterprises democratically owned and controlled by employees, with the government encouraging, through generous credit and other provisions, the establishment of producer and consumer cooperatives, "small-scale, de-alienating, good for training workers in running their own affairs."[11]

Such a bundle of reforms, graduated in their social penetration, would signify a radical series of changes, even if not yet reaching a socialist society. One lesson to be learned from past efforts of socialist governments is that much depends on pacing. Too slow a rate of change disappoints enthusiastic followers; too rapid can lead to the loss of middle-class support, excessive inflation (there is bound to be some), and serious disturbances. Choices would have to be made, so that fundamental socioeconomic measures would not be jeopardized by divisions over secondary or symbolic issues. And a socialist government, it should be remembered, would also have a stake in maintaining a good measure of national cohesion and civility, even if its legislation antagonized large property owners and small ideologues.

Such transitional measures, whatever their ultimate benefits, are certain to create immediate difficulties. Substantial benefits for the poorest segments of the population—absolutely; but if on too lavish a scale, these can result in an inflation threatening both the economic program and the political stability of the government. Sweeping tax reforms—desirable; but if too sweeping, they can alienate segments of the middle class whose support a socialist government needs. A wealth tax—attractive; but it can lead to capital flight. Economic controls—probably unavoidable; but they entail the likelihood of shortages, black markets, misallocation of resources, economic imbalances.

One suggested way of alleviating these difficulties would be to stress the need for higher productivity, "a larger pie," so that most segments of the population would be satisfied with immediate benefits. But it's by no means certain that in a transitional period this could be achieved. And such proposals for economic growth would encounter a bumpy course: they would be opposed by people who feared the ecological consequences and thought "consumerism" at variance with the socialist ethos, as well as by entrepreneurs and managers reluctant to help raise productivity at the very moment their "prerogatives" were being curbed. At least with regard to the managers, however, an imaginative government would work very hard to gain their cooperation, arguing that many of them, especially at middle levels, had no unalterable stake in perpetuating corporate control of economic life or in vast social inequities.

A democratic commitment—unconditional as it is and must be—may well constrain, delay, and even thwart socialist programs. Socialist governments do not rest on undifferentiated popular support, and many of their voters might not wish them to go beyond limited reforms. Socialist governments must put into office people who lack experience and often, in consequence, make mistakes or slip into caution, even confusion. Socialist governments need to find channels to capital growth, but the tensions created by the changes they initiate can lead to panic and "sabotage" in capital markets. And even the best-conceived program of transition is likely to be hostage to the business cycle, as well as to imbalances of wealth and power among the nations.

A painful irony must here be acknowledged: many of the criticisms Leninists have made of social-democratic reformism have a point; for instance, that timidity would inhibit radical initiatives while radical excess could drive people of the political and social middle to become outright opponents. The Leninist conclusion is that the "transition period" requires a "temporary" abrogation of democracy, in the name, to be sure, of a "higher democracy." This cure, however, is far worse than any malady one can imagine, since "temporary" dictatorships have a way of slipping into permanence, especially those established by communist parties, and, what's more, they usually fail to cope with the economic problems they alone are supposedly able to solve.

There is no undemocratic road to socialism; there are only undemocratic roads that can bring, and have brought, nations to barbaric mockeries of the socialist idea. If we were forced to conclude that there cannot be a democratic road to socialism, then we would also have to conclude that the entire socialist enterprise is illusory.

We understand now—experience must teach us *something*—that the transition from capitalism to socialism is likely to be a lengthy process, interrupted by setbacks, and fraught with tensions, conflicts, difficulties, and errors. But if it is to be a socialism of free men and women, there can be no other way.

5.

Between the period of "transition" and a "full" or achieved socialism there is no thick or impenetrable wall. The distinction is mostly an analytical convenience. A healthy society must always be in transition; a dynamic socialism can never be "full."

What, then, would the social structure of a democratic-socialist society look like? Mulling over this question, I find myself in some sympathy with the traditional leftist reluctance to indulge in "future-painting." Certainly there can be no call, at this point in history, for either prediction or prescription. But, also, it is too late to trust simply to the workings of history; tokens must be offered of the *direction* in which we hope to move, even if, and perhaps especially if, there is no immediate possibility of reaching the desired goal.

But must not any discussion of a socialist society now seem remote, unrelated to current needs and concerns? It all depends on the spirit and terms in which we approach the matter. Everyone knows that today in the United States socialism is not on the political agenda; but can anyone be certain that there will not be new or recurrent social crises that will give an unexpected relevance to at least some of the basic socialist proposals? Within or close to a number of European socialist parties there are significant groups of political people that are seriously trying to sketch out "the face of socialism." Though involved in powerful parties, these people also know that a socialist transformation is not on the immediate agenda in Europe. But they understand that, in view of the volatility of modern history and the appearance of unexpected possibilities, it is necessary to think now with regard to what may be done the day after tomorrow. (And perhaps the day after tomorrow will come—tomorrow.) There is, furthermore, one great advantage in being powerless, and that is that it enables, sometimes stimulates, serious thought. Re-establishing socialism as an idea is not a sufficient, but it is surely a necessary, condition for re-establishing it as a dynamic politics. So, with all the necessary qualifications as to tentativeness and speculativeness, I proceed to offer a sketch of a sketch, cheerfully pilfered from the work of several recent writers.*

---

*Among them Oscar Lange, Abram Bergson, George Lichtheim, Radoslav Selucky, Henry Pachter, Wlodzimierz Brus, Michael Harrington, and Alec Nove.

Let us focus on two models for a democratic socialism offered by Radoslav Selucky, a Czech exile now living in the West, and Alec Nove, an economist living in Scotland. As a matter of strict principle, both agree on the need for multiparty democracy. Anything remotely like the centralized "command economies" of Eastern Europe must be entirely avoided, since these are economically inept, politically repressive, and intellectually intolerable.* Both writers agree also on the need for a market economy, subject to controls by a democratic polity. Laissez-faire would be quite as inoperative under advanced socialism as it has turned out to be under advanced capitalism. Where they differ significantly is with regard to structures of property and productive relations in a "market socialism." Selucky strongly favors social controls from below, whereas Nove would encourage a greater variety in the modes of ownership. I suppose that Selucky's views on this matter are more attractive and Nove's more realistic.

Selucky lists a number of concise premises for his model, the essential ones of which I quote:

---

*The centralized, authoritarian structure of the East European societies "requires that all basic economic decisions be made at the top of the social hierarchy. Because the producers are dispersed, of technological necessity, the basic division of labor between those who rule, control, plan and manage, and those who are ruled, controlled, planned and managed, cannot but remain in existence despite the nationalization of the means of production. From the functional point of view, it is irrelevant who has a formal title to property; *what is relevant is who disposes of it, who decides on it, who manipulates it, in whose interest one makes decisions and in whose interest controlling functions are exercised. . . .*"[12]

> The means of production are owned socially and managed by those who make use of them.
>
> Social ownership of the means of production is separated from the state.
>
> Producing and trading enterprises are autonomous from the state and independent of each other. They operate within the framework of the market which is regulated by a central indicative plan.
>
> The institutions which provide health, education and welfare services are wholly exempt from the market.
>
> The right to participate in direct management of the work units *operating in the market* is derived from labor.
>
> The right to participate in direct management of the work units *exempt wholly or partly from the market* is derived proportionally from labor, ownership, and consumption of the provided services and utilities.
>
> The right to participate in indirect political control over, and regulation of, the socially owned means of production is derived from one's position as a citizen.
>
> Health and education services and social benefits for the disabled are distributed according to one's needs.
>
> Economic equality consists of each individual's equal access to the means of production, health and education services, social benefits and self-management [in economic enterprises]. Since it does not include egalitarian distribution of income, individuals —while equal in essence—are unequal in their existence.
>
> The principle of self-management is limited to microeconomic units only.[13]

This model seems attractive in several respects. It stresses—as, after the experiences of our century, socialists must stress—the separation of political and economic power. It proposes a dispersal of economic power in horizontal enterprises, each largely self-sustaining and freely administered, though subject both to market signals and social regulation. It provides consumers with freedom of choice, and citizens with free occupational and educational choices. It favors a market mechanism that would be interdependent with "indicative" planning—that is, planning not merely imposed from above but with institutional mechanisms for democratic decision-making and checks from below. And it rests on direct democracy within the workplace insofar as that is possible, and on representative democracy in the society as a whole.

This model presupposes the flourishing of "civil society" and its autonomous "secondary institutions" (trade unions, political groups, fraternal societies, etc.) apart from and, when necessary, in opposition to the state. The intent is clearly to make possible a pluralist flexibility that is present in, though often only claimed for, capitalist democracy, while at the same time eliminating many of its socially retrogressive features.

In such a socialist society, wage levels would be subject to the law of supply and demand, shaped in part through collective bargaining undertaken by free trade unions, though also (as is sometimes now true in industrial nations) bounded by social regulations such as "incomes policies." Wage differentials would remain, in accordance with pressures of scarcity and skill, though again subject to social boundaries. The market would provide goods and services; it would regulate prices, except for those controlled as part of public policy and those products the society might decide to provide without cost. And while in its initial phases a democratic-socialist society would have to strive for increases in production and higher productivity, it might after a time, through modest increments, supersede the efficiency principle in behalf of more attractive social ends.*

---

*In such a society, observes Abram Bergson, "managers of socialist plants and industries—the former responsible primarily for current

Alec Nove's model for democratic socialism differs from Selucky's in one crucial respect. Selucky, writes Nove,

> appears to envisage an evolution toward one type of producing unit. In my view it is possible and desirable to have several. . . . It is essential to recall the assumptions of political democracy. The citizens can choose, for example, what sorts of private initiative to encourage or to tolerate, the desirable forms of cooperatives, the extent of workers' participation in management, and much else besides. They can experiment, learn from experience, commit and correct errors. . . . Suppose that we have a legal structure which permits the following species:
>
> 1. State enterprises, centrally controlled and administered, hereinafter [called] *centralized state corporations.*
> 2. State-owned (or socially-owned) enterprises with full autonomy and a management responsible to the workforce, hereinafter [called] *socialized enterprises.*
> 3. *Cooperative enterprises.*
> 4. *Small-scale private enterprise,* subject to clearly defined limits.
> 5. *Individuals* (e.g., freelance journalists, plumbers, artists).[15]

---

operations, the latter for larger investments, especially introduction of new plants—are allowed similarly to determine autonomously inputs of factors and corresponding outputs. In the process, however, each is supposed to observe two rules: 1) to combine factors in such a way as to assure that at the prices established for such inputs any given output is produced at a minimum cost, and 2) to fix the scale of output of any commodity produced at a point where its marginal cost equals the corresponding price."[14]

The idea of a greater diversity of production units is in principle appealing, since the aim of a socialist society ought to be the maximizing of opportunity, choice, and freedom as long as these remain within democratically agreed-upon bounds. The "centralized state corporations" would include, besides banks, enterprises that are necessarily very large or occupy a monopoly position, or both—where significant economies of scale can be realized. Among examples of such "state corporations" are power stations, and oil and petrochemical complexes. But the criterion here ought to be technological, not the corporate structure that prevails today, since some present-day corporations are large because of the power it gives them over the market, rather than because of any criteria of efficiency. A danger might arise that some of these giant enterprises would assume a monopoly posture under socialism as disadvantageous to consumers and workers as under capitalism. To rein in such enterprises, both of our models envisage "tripartite management" (government, consumers, workers).

In the socialized and cooperative enterprises, according to the Nove model, managers would be appointed by an elected committee representing the employees and would be responsible to that committee for basic policy. One main difference between socialized and cooperative enterprises is that in the former the state would have "a residual responsibility for their use or misuse, or for debts incurred," whereas a cooperative could freely dispose of its property or decide to go out of business (again, no doubt, within the bounds of social regulations). As for small-scale private enterprise,

> Presumably even the fanatical dogmatist would accept the existence of freelance writers, painters and dressmakers. My own list would be longer. Indeed, there should be no list. If any activity

> (not actually a "social bad" in itself) can be fruitfully and profitably undertaken by any individual, this sets up the presumption of its legitimacy. . . . So long as it is one individual, there would probably be no objection. . . . But there would be also the possibility of a private entrepreneur actually employing a few people, which makes him an "exploiter" insofar as he makes a profit out of their work. . . .
>
> Subject to limits, this should be allowed.
>
> Subject to what limits? This could be decided democratically in the light of circumstances and experience. The limit could be on numbers employed, or on the value of capital assets, and could be varied by sector. One possible rule might be that above this limit there be a choice, either to convert into a cooperative or to become a socialized enterprise, with proper compensation for the original entrepreneur. . . . Be it noted that there is no provision for any class of capitalists; our small private entrepreneur *works,* even when employing a few others. There is then no *unearned* income, arising simply from *ownership* of capital or land.[16]

Scale as well as structure is important. The larger the enterprise, the more difficult self-management becomes and the more likely its bureaucratic deformation. But I do not see why even in subdivisions of Nove's "centralized state enterprises" there could not be nurtured at least a measure of workers' control regarding such matters as relations to and pace of work, even if it is granted that on large overall decisions (how much oil Britain should extract from the North Sea) there would have to be vertical decision-making subject to the check of the democratic polity.

In Nove's model the extent of central planning is, then, greater than in Selucky's. Making major investment decisions; monitoring decentralized investments; administering such "naturally" central productive activities as electricity, oil, railways (today "public," actually private, utilities); setting ground rules for the autonomous economic sectors, "with reserve powers of intervention when things got out of balance" (today bailing out Chrysler, Penn Central); drafting long-term plans—all these, subject to decision and check by parliament or congress, would be the responsibility of central planning, thus entailing a greater concentration of economic power than many socialists, myself included, would prefer. But who can say with assurance? One encounters here a deep and inescapable tension between the technological-economic realm and the democratic-social arrangements of a socialist (perhaps any modern) society. Mediating between these forces would become a major responsibility for both state and society, government and the people, in a free socialist order.

In all such projected arrangements a crucial factor must surely be the morale and consciousness of the people. It isn't necessary, or desirable, to envisage a constant state of intense participation in public affairs, a noisy turmoil of activists, in order to recognize that the felt quality—as distinct from the mere economic workability—of such a society would depend on the fundamental concern of a sizable portion of the population. "No social system," Joseph Schumpeter has remarked, "can work that is based exclusively upon a network of free contracts . . . and in which everyone is supposed to be guided by nothing except his own (short-run) utilitarian ends."[17] True for any democratic society, this would be all the more true for one aspiring to realize socialist ideals.

If put to the test of reality, such projections would surely require many changes. But the purpose of this sort of model is not to "appropriate" the future; it is to indicate the nature of thought in the present. Nor need it be denied that such models contain within themselves a good many unresolved problems, tensions, perhaps even contradictions. They *should* contain them, for that is what lends a savor of reality. Let me now, in no particular order, consider a few of these problems:

• The Selucky and Nove models of ownership suffer from opposite difficulties. Selucky's lacks variety and flexibility in its proposals: why should there not be a range of democratic structures in economic life just as there is in political life? Nove's model, by contrast, gives an uncomfortably strong place to "centralized state corporations." The ogre of bureaucratism rises with regard to both—in opposite ways, the one through rigidity and the other through concentration. In principle one would like to combine Selucky's stress upon worker self-management with Nove's stress upon varieties of property, but that may be asking for the best of all possible worlds, something actuality is chary of providing.

• Neither of our model-makers discusses sufficiently one major problem: the place of unions in a democratic-socialist society. If the workers own an enterprise cooperatively or if they manage one democratically, is there still a need for unions? I would say yes, unambiguously. Insofar as we think of a socialist society as one with autonomous institutions and enterprises, this entails the likelihood and even desirability of democratically contained conflict; and insofar as there is conflict, the weaker segments of the population should be able to protect themselves through organization. It's possible to foresee a situation in which a minority of workers in a self-managed enterprise believes it is being mistreated by the majority; that minority thereupon organizes itself into something very much like a union. In the "centralized state corporations" that Nove proposes as one mode of socialist ownership, there would surely be a need for strong unions to resist bureaucratic dictate. As for cooperatives, take the example of the Israeli kibbutzim. They function pretty much like cooperatives, but also hire outside labor at wage rates; the people so hired may well feel they need a union to protect themselves against the benign or not-so-benign edicts of the cooperatives. So it could be in many areas of a socialist society. A pluralism of institutions signifies a plurality of interests, and these must express themselves openly through modulated conflict-and-cooperation.

• It would be hard, according to the economist Abram Bergson, to work out satisfactory criteria of success and reward for managers of the autonomous productive units in a socialist society. Pressed by the often clashing interests of the worker-employers and the central planning agencies of the state, managers might hesitate to take risks or use their initiative. They would need, also, to adjudicate between local interests and larger, more distant social goals, which might put them in a crossfire and cause them to yield to whichever side was the strongest. Incentives would have to be attached to their jobs, allowing them sufficient authority to display leadership while still subjecting them to the democratic check of worker-employers. In cases of major disputes, decisions would have to be referred to the next-highest level of authority, perhaps an industry-wide council.

• Nor is it difficult to foresee conflicts among autonomous enterprises as they compete for the credits, subsidies, tax breaks, and contracts that are to be had from the state. Just as, under capitalism, competition tends to destroy competition, so it is by no means excluded that self-managed enterprises can form rings or cartels. This would have to be resisted except perhaps in circumstances where economies of scale are *very* substantial. It might even be necessary to introduce a species of "socialist anti-trust" legislation. For until the society reached an unforeseeable state of material abundance, a major source of conflict could well be that between general and partial interests, society as a whole and its regions, social groups and industrial units.

As Selucky says very sensibly, "Since no [complete] harmony of interests is possible at every level of society," there would have to be mediators to control the conflicting interests. "To regulate the conflicts, two mediators are necessary: the market mechanism for economics and the multi-party system for politics."[18]

• Employment and income policies could also bring serious difficulties—for instance, coping with tendencies toward local monopolizing of jobs where enterprise profits are high; working out income policies that might arouse opposition from unions but could be seen as justifiable for the common good; finding ways to help workers whom technological changes in a given industry or enterprise have rendered superfluous; deciding upon—or establishing criteria for deciding upon—appropriate surpluses for capital investments and new technologies as against the "natural" inclination of self-managed communities to reap immediate rewards, etc. For that matter, it is foolhardy to suppose that unemployment might not be a problem in a democratic-socialist society: all one can reasonably expect is a readiness to deal with it quickly and fairly.

• Another complex of problems worth at least pointing to concerns how, when, and whether the state should intervene if a self-managed enterprise is failing. For some would fail, the operation of even a regulated market under socialism having some parallels to its operation under capitalism.

- Many such problems constitute disadvantages probably inseparable from the advantages of a regulated market, and they seem to reinforce the traditional critiques, both Marxist and romantic, of the market. That the market subjects the human encounter to the fetishism of commodities, signifying that men are not entirely free from the rule of impersonal exchange and wage labor, is true. But unless we can suppose an implausible cornucopia of goods and services, we had better accept the idea of a regulated market as necessary under a feasible democratic socialism.

A socially controlled market would also have some attractive features. The argument against capitalism first made by R. H. Tawney still holds—not that it's bad if people take some risks but that in a society where a few have much and most have little or nothing, the majority doesn't enjoy the privilege of taking risks. Risk, thought Tawney, is "bracing if it is voluntarily undertaken," and in a cooperative commonwealth, self-managed enterprises and producers' cooperatives could take socially useful risks that would bring into play their energies and minds.

Still, the market has the drawbacks traditionally noted by the left, and one possible way of getting past some of these, as also perhaps moving a bit closer to Marx's vision of "free associated producers," is a modest increase in society's provision of free goods. Some commodities could be produced in such abundance and at so small a cost, it would be economical to dispose of them at zero price rather than incur the overhead costs of charging for them. Even today, some health and many educational services are free, which in actuality means they are carried as a shared or social cost. In a cooperative commonwealth, such provision might be extended to milk, perhaps even bread. Would people take more than they need, would there be waste at first? Probably; yet that might not be so wasteful as many of the practices we simply take for granted in a capitalist society. And as free access to a modest number of basic goods became customary, misuse of the privilege would probably decrease. Nevertheless, in a market socialism such free provision could only be marginal.

• All of these problems are instances of a larger problem often cited by conservatives, for whom socialism is anathema, as the market is for doctrinal Marxists. It is possible that the autonomous enterprises might repeat some of the socially undesirable behavior with which we are familiar in corporate capitalism, functioning as "socialist corporate" units in quite as selfish a spirit as present-day corporations are known to do. When doctrinaire leftists (or rightists, for that matter) point to possible abuses in a market socialism, they are almost always pointing to risks present in any democratic society. Mistakes and abuses are always with us; this is a condition of freedom and can be eliminated only by eliminating freedom itself.

Think back to the alliance between monopoly capital and street lumpens that enabled the Nazis to come to power in Germany. The risk there was extreme; steps could have been taken, within democratic limits, to minimize it, but no one in his senses would suggest that the Weimar republic should have been destroyed in order to avoid the rise of Nazism. Or consider the enormous power that corporate wealth exerts in America today: whatever the remedy, it is surely not to eliminate democratic procedures.

What would be needed in a democratic-socialist society (as today in a democratic-capitalist society) is some version of the welfare state. Through electoral decisions, compromises, and bargaining, it could adjudicate among conflicting parts of the population, setting rules for the operation of the market while protecting both the norms of the society and the rights of its citizens.

6.

Finally, the socialist aspiration has less to do with modes of property ownership than with qualities of social life. That is why the case for socialism rests not just on its proposed reduction of inequities in wealth and power, but on its wish to democratize economic practice. The two values—equality and freedom—are sometimes, of course, in tension, but when regarded in a spirit of generosity and humaneness, they flourish together, as they seem to have flourished during the early days of the American republic.

The egalitarian ideal has been very strong in socialist thought and tradition. It should be. There is something morally repulsive in the maldistribution of wealth and income in a country like the United States. And this state of affairs is not only morally repulsive but also socially unjust, a major barrier to the genuine realization of the democratic idea. Now, any proposal can be pushed too far, turning into a vicious parody of itself. An egalitarianism enforced by authoritarian decree—what's called in Eastern Europe "barracks egalitarianism"—is something utterly alien to the socialist idea. Our vision of egalitarianism implies a steady, perhaps slow, and surely gradual rectification of inequities through education, legislation, and popular assent; it aims not for some absurd version of total equality (whatever that might mean) but, rather, for a progress toward the fair sharing of socioeconomic goods and political power, which would allow each person to fulfill his or her potentialities.

One precondition is both political and economic democracy, with the latter signifying the replacement, insofar as possible, of "vertical," hierarchical structures by "horizontal," egalitarian ones. Workers' control, self-management by those who work in an enterprise—some such concept is crucial to the socialist hope. One needn't be a fanatic and set up standards so impossibly high that they will fall of their own weight. But in the end socialists have no choice but to accept the wager—either a genuine, if imperfect, economic democracy is realizable or the entire socialist enterprise must be relegated to historical fantasy.

No longer tolerating their reduction to mere factors of production, workers would learn through experience to demand their rights as free, autonomous men and women. They would form cooperatives. They would acquire some of the skills of management (those arcane mysteries, it's sometimes said, which must forever remain beyond the reach of the lowly). And in time there could be a tradeoff between some of the efficiencies brought about (allegedly) by authoritarian forms of organization and the growing creativity of cooperative production.

Too often in recent socialist literature the idea, sometimes merely the slogan, of workers' control has remained gloriously vague. What does it mean precisely? That decisions regarding production, prices, wages, and investment in a giant enterprise like a "socialist GM" would be made by the assembled workers or even their representatives? And if so, how would it be possible to avoid the linked plagues of bureaucratism, demagogic manipulation, clique maneuverings, endless filibustering, ignorant narrowness, cronyism in elections, and a selfish resistance to the larger needs of society?

One frequent argument against self-management proposals is that their advocates tend to minimize the sheer complexity of modern enterprise. Laymen (workers) would have difficulty in securing relevant information from managers; they would often be unable to grasp the technical aspects of the information they got; and they would lack the time needed to reflect upon what they did grasp in order to arrive at coherent plans. There is of course some truth to this argument, though it largely proceeds on the assumption that workers in a better society will remain quite as workers are today. But there is reason to expect that with higher levels of education and a greater provision for time, leisure, and training within the organized work community, some of these problems could be overcome. Lethargy isn't a universal constant; it is a socially conditioned phenomenon open to change. "Full" participation in managerial activities might, in some situations, turn out to be a chimera; but there surely could be a large measure of selective control by workers, even in giant enterprises, with technicalities left to managers and large policy issues decided through democratic mechanisms.

A somewhat different problem is raised in a recent study by Allen Graubard, who sees workers' control, narrowly conceived, as clashing with public rights. A large corporation "is a national resource. . . . The same argument against private control of the founder-owner or by the current corporate owner works . . . against private control by the community of employees. The authority for major decisions of the enterprise should rest in the larger public, the democratic polity."[19]

This criticism can best be regarded as a warning against *exclu-*

sive control of major enterprises by the workers within them—though even that should not preclude a good measure of self-management with regard to intraplant arrangements. About such matters it would be foolish to be dogmatic; far better to recognize a multiplicity of interests and outlooks, with the certainty that, if ventures in self-management are undertaken, they will be subject to many difficulties.

The practical impediments to workers' self-management that both sophisticated organization theorists and "the man in the street" detect are often real enough—but are the consequent objections very much more cogent than similar arguments once used against the feasibility of political democracy?

The excrescence of bureaucratism might indeed flourish on the structure of self-management. Who in the twentieth century can deny that possibility (or *any* possibility)? Here everything depends on conscious effort, that vigilance which had better be eternal—quite as with regard to political democracy. And there is much cogency in an argument advanced by George Lichtheim that

> A future advance will probably have to start from a concept of technical education which envisages it not simply as a means of improving efficiency, but as a link between the worker and the planner. . . . For the worker technology holds the most direct access to science and everything that lies beyond it. But technical education without responsible participation soon loses its spur. . . . For [socialists], its significance . . . lies in the fact that it arises spontaneously out of the modern process of work, while at the same time it enables the worker to develop his individuality.[20]

In practice, self-management would sometimes thrive, sometimes stumble, but always be marked, like all human enterprises, by imperfections. There is one argument, however, against self-management that seems to me peculiarly insidious: it is offered, as you might expect, by ex-radicals, and its main thrust is that workers "show little interest" in the idea.

In certain empirical respects, this is not even true. Through their unions, workers have often fought very hard for such noneconomic rights as grievance mechanisms and proper work atmospheres. These inroads on traditional "management prerogatives" often constitute modest beginnings of economic democracy, whether or not those who make the inroads so conceptualize them. Still, for the sake of the argument, let us grant the conservative claim that workers today "show little interest" in self-management proposals. To stop there would be supinely to acquiesce in "the given." For this argument against self-management is essentially an extension of a larger skepticism about democratic politics. How often have we not heard that most people care more about their bellies than their freedoms? Or that in the United States millions of citizens don't even bother to vote? Notions of self-management, our conservatives tell us, are mere futile efforts by small groups of intellectuals to "impose their fantasies" upon ordinary people who seem quite content to allow the corporations to determine their work lives.

Few of us are born passionate democrats. The values of freedom have to be learned. Centuries passed before masses of men came to feel that democracy is a necessity of life. All the while it was a not-very-large company of intellectuals who sought to "impose their fantasies" about democracy upon ordinary people. Even today, who can say that this persuasion has taken deep enough root?

It may be a long time before the value of democratic norms is secured in socioeconomic life. An independent Yugoslav writer, Branko Horvat, reports that in his country "inherited authoritarian attitudes are so deeply ingrained that they are unconsciously carried into self-management."[21] Could it be otherwise, especially in a country with little experience in political democracy, before or after Tito?

Nothing is ordained. Socialism, self-management, economic democracy are options, sometimes brighter, sometimes dimmer. The realization of the socialist hope depends on the growth of consciousness, a finer grasp of the possibilities of citizenship and comradeship than now prevails. Times change. We will emerge from our present slough of small-spirited conservative acquiescence and live again by more generous aspirations. The idea of self-management could then take a somewhat more prominent place on the agenda of public discourse—kept alive by "unrealistic intellectuals," "visionary socialists."

7.

Amid such turnings and reassessment of political thought, a harsh question intrudes itself: Does the socialist idea, even if rendered more sophisticated than it was in the past, still survive as a significant option? Has it outlived its historical moment?

Socialist movements have great achievements to their credit, yet nowhere on the globe can one point to a free, developed socialist society. The proclaimed goal has not been reached, and as I write it does not seem close. Socialism has been shaken by failures, torn by doubts. Its language and symbols have been appropriated by parodic totalitarianism, and from this trauma we have still to recover.

Historical energy and idealism cannot be supplied on demand. Once an idea becomes contaminated or a generation exhausted, it is a long time before new energies can be summoned, if summoned at all. Whether socialism can be revived as a living idea—which is something different from the mere survival of European social-democratic parties as established institutions—is by now very much a question. So too is the possibility, or hope, that socialism may serve as a bridge toward a radical new humanism. In any case, socialists remain. They engage themselves with the needs of the moment, struggling for betterment in matters large and small, reforms major and modest: they do not sit and wait for the millennium. And they continue also to grapple with fragments of a tradition.

This intellectual effort, it must be admitted, can handicap them politically. Not many people became socialists because they were persuaded of the correctness of Marxist economics or supposed the movement served their "class interests." They became socialists because they were moved to fervor by the call to brotherhood and sisterhood; because the world seemed aglow with the vision of a time in which humanity might live in justice and peace. Whatever we may now claim for a refurbished socialism, we can hardly claim that it satisfies the emotions as once the early movement did.

If it is true that utopian-apocalyptic expectations are indispensable to a movement advocating major social change, then democratic socialists are in deeper trouble than even they recognize. For in politics, as elsewhere, choices must be made. You cannot opt for the rhythms of a democratic politics and still expect it to yield the pathos and excitement of revolutionary movements. Our hope must be that there are other kinds of fervor—quieter, less melodramatic, morally stronger—which a democratic reformist politics can evoke.

Modern postindustrial society, with its relatively high levels of culture and education, may enable a politics offering proposals for major social change while also avoiding the delusions of "total" transformation. A liberal socialism, at once pragmatic and idealistic, may yet be able to win the loyalties of a new public, cutting across class lines and appealing to the best in humanity.

I have been speaking about the problem of socialism as if it were self-sufficient and self-referential; but that is no more than a useful analytic device, an abstraction from the real world, in which the fate of socialism must be bound up with the fate of capitalism. We cannot be certain. The recovery of Western capitalism during the several decades after World War II has come to a halt; there is clearly a serious crisis in the West regarding such problems as unemployment, technological change, relations with the underdeveloped world, etc.; and how well democratic capitalism will be able to cope with these problems is very much a question. Socialists make their proposals for coping with such problems, and the revival of their movement depends in good measure on the cogency and passion with which they offer ways of dealing with immediate human needs, as well as the persuasiveness of the good society they try to sketch.

Our problem may be restated as that of utopianism—does the utopian vision still have value for us?

The "utopia" imposed through force and terror by a self-chosen vanguard is hell. The utopia of a "withering away of the state" is a fantasy gone stale. But there remains a utopian outlook that relates immediate objectives to ultimate goals, and it is to this that socialists cling. As Leszek Kolakowski has written: ". . . goals now unattainable will never be reached unless they are articulated when they are still unattainable. . . . The existence of a utopia as a utopia is the necessary prerequisite for its eventually ceasing to be a utopia."[22]

"Very nice," a friendly voice interjects, "but socialism—has not that name been soiled in the pillagings of our century? Might it not be better for a movement to shake itself clear of all the old confusions, defeats, betrayals?"

I can well imagine that a movement in America might choose to drop the socialist label: who needs, once again, to explain that we do *not* want the kinds of society that exist in Russia and China, Poland and Cuba? But, at least with regard to America, we continue to speak of small groups trying to keep alive a tradition. Suppose, indeed, we were to conclude that the socialist label creates more trouble than it's worth: we would then have to cast about for a new vocabulary, something not to be won through fiat. How much would actually change if our words were to change? If, say, we ceased calling ourselves socialists and instead announced that henceforth we are to be known as—what? "Economic democrats" or "democratic radicals"? The substance of our problems would remain, the weight of this century's burdens still press upon us. We would still regard capitalist society as an unjust society, still find intolerable its inequities, still be repelled by its ethic of greed, and still be trying to sketch the outlines of a better society.

Isaiah Berlin has written that liberalism is "a notoriously exposed, dangerous, and ungrateful position." I would borrow his words for democratic socialism, which is not quite the same as but, in my sense of things, has a kinship with his liberalism.

For those socialists who have experienced in their bones the meaning of our century, the time has not yet come, I believe, to cast off its burdens. Such a time may come. Meanwhile, we hope to serve as a link to those friends of tomorrow who will have so completely absorbed the lessons of our age that they will not need to rehearse them. Whatever the fate of socialism, the yearning for a better mode of life which found expression in its thought and its struggle will reappear. Of that I am absolutely certain.

Notes

The Era of Debs

1. James R. Green, *Grass-Roots Socialism: Radical Movements in the Southwest, 1895–1943* (Baton Rouge, La., 1978), p. xx.

2. James R. Green, "Populism, Socialism and the Promise of Democracy," *Radical History Review,* fall 1980, p. 18.

3. Oscar Ameringer, *If You Don't Weaken: The Autobiography of Oscar Ameringer* (New York, 1940), pp. 263–66.

4. James Weinstein, *The Decline of Socialism in America, 1912–1925* (New York, 1969), pp. 13–14.

5. Eugene V. Debs, "Sound Socialist Tactics," *International Socialist Review,* February 1912, p. 483.

6. Nick Salvatore, *Eugene V. Debs, Citizen and Socialist* (Urbana, Ill., 1982), p. 225.

7. Quoted in R. Laurence Moore, "Flawed Fraternity—American Socialist Response to the Negro, 1901–1912," *The Historian,* November 1969, p. 8.

8. Eugene V. Debs, "The Negro in the Class Struggle," *International Socialist Review,* November 1903, p. 260.

9. Quoted in Moore, "Flawed Fraternity," p. 15.

10. Weinstein, *Decline of Socialism,* p. 32.

11. John Laslett, *Labor and the Left* (New York, 1970), p. 271.

12. Quoted in Carl Degler, *Out of Our Past* (New York, 1959), p. 266.

13. Daniel Bell, *Marxian Socialism in the United States* (Princeton, N. J., 1967), p. 44.

14. Salvatore, *Eugene V. Debs,* p. 237.

15. E. P. Thompson, *The Making of the English Working Class* (New York, 1964), p. 394.

16. Daniel Bell, "The Problem of Ideological Rigidity," in John H. M. Laslett and Seymour Martin Lipset, eds., *Failure of a Dream? Essays in the History of American Socialism* (New York, 1974), p. 89.

17. William English Walling, *Progressivism and After* (New York, 1914), p. 22.

18. Walter Lippmann, "On Municipal Socialism, 1913," reprinted in Bruce M. Stave, ed., *Socialism and the Cities* (Port Washington, N.Y., 1975), pp. 189, 195.

19. Green, *Grass-Roots Socialism,* pp. 349, 350, 365.

20. Sally Miller, *Victor Berger and the Promise of Constructive Socialism* (Westport, Conn., 1973), p. 160.

21. Gerald Friedberg, "Comment," in Laslett and Lipset, eds., *Failure of a Dream?,* p. 348.

22. Quoted in Weinstein, *Decline of Socialism,* p. 181.

Socialists in the Thirties

1. From an unpublished interview with Clarence Senior, by Harry Fleischman, March 1974, courtesy of Mr. Fleischman.

2. Ibid.

3. Morris Hillquit, "Problems Before the National Convention," *American Socialist Quarterly,* April 1932, p. 9.

4. Quoted in W. A. Swanberg, *Norman Thomas: The Last Idealist* (New York, 1976), p. 148.

5. Ibid., p. 148.

6. Letter of Norman Thomas to M. S. Vekataramani, quoted in latter's "United Front Tactics of the Communist Party, USA and Their Impact on the Socialist Party of America, 1932–6," *International Studies* I, no. 2 (October 1959), p. 159.

7. Quoted in *New York Times,* February 17, 1934.

8. *New Leader,* February 24, 1934.

9. Socialist Party newspaper, April 13, 1933.

10. Quoted in Greg Mitchell, "Summer of '34," *Working Papers,* November-December 1982, p. 26.

11. Ibid., p. 29.

12. Alan Brinkley, *Voices of Protest* (New York, 1982), p. 239.

13. Quoted in Swanberg, *Norman Thomas,* p. 152.

14. Reinhold Niebuhr, "The Revolutionary Moment," *American Socialist Quarterly,* June 1935, p. 9.

15. Quoted in Daniel Bell, *Marxian Socialism in the United States* (Princeton, N.J., 1967), p. 166.

16. Transcript, National Convention, Socialist Party, 1934.

17. Ibid.

18. David Shannon, *The Socialist Party of America* (Chicago, 1967), p. 248.

19. Norman Thomas, *A Socialist Looks at the New Deal,* pamphlet, League for Industrial Democracy, 1933, p. 4.

20. Norman Thomas, *The Choice Before Us* (New York, 1934), p. 92.

21. Norman Thomas, "Is the New Deal Socialism?," text of radio speech over Columbia Broadcasting System, February 2, 1936, published as pamphlet by Socialist Party.

22. James R. Green, *Grass-Roots Socialism: Radical Movements in the Southwest, 1895–1943* (Baton Rouge, La., 1978), p. 424.

23. Richard Hofstadter, *The American Political Tradition* (New York, 1948), p. 340.

24. Swanberg, *Norman Thomas,* p. 201.

25. Powers Hapgood papers, University of Indiana Library.

26. Ibid.

27. Letter of Norman Thomas to Ben [Fischer] and Tucker [Smith], August 19, 1938.

The Brilliant Masquerade: A Note on "Browderism"

1. Harvey Klehr, *The Heyday of American Communism* (New York, 1984), p. 190.

2. Ibid., p. 257.

3. The material in this paragraph is taken from Irving Howe and Lewis Coser, *The American Communist Party: A Critical History* (Boston, 1957), chap. VIII.

Why Has Socialism Failed in America?

1. Engels letter, August 7, 1851, *Letters to Americans, 1848–1895* (New York, 1953), pp. 25–26.

2. Marx letter, March 5, 1852, ibid., pp. 44–45.

3. Quoted in R. Laurence Moore, *European Socialists and the American Promised Land* (New York, 1970), p. 9.

4. Marx letter, June 20, 1881, *Letters to Americans,* p. 129.

5. Engels's Preface, *The Civil War in France,* 1891 ed. (Chicago, 1934), p. 24.

6. Engels, *The Condition of the Working Class in England* (1887 ed.).

7. Engels letter, December 2, 1893, *Letters to Americans,* p. 258.

8. Quoted in Russell Jacoby, "Politics of the Crisis Theory," *Telos,* spring 1975, p. 7.

9. Ibid., p. 8.

10. Daniel Bell, *Marxian Socialism in the United States* (Princeton, N.J., 1967), p. 5.

11. Louis Hartz, "Reply," in John H. M. Laslett and Seymour Martin Lipset, eds., *Failure of a Dream? Essays in the History of American Socialism* (Garden City, N.Y., 1974), p. 421.

12. V. I. Lenin, Appendix, *Letters to Americans,* p. 275.

13. Engels letter, February 8, 1890, in *Karl Marx and Friedrich Engels: Selected Correspondence, 1846–1895* (New York, 1942), p. 467.

14. Engels, *Letters to Americans,* Appendix, p. 287.

15. Werner Sombart, *Why Is There No Socialism in the United States?,* ed. C. T. Husbands (White Plains, N.Y., 1976), p. 18.

16. Ibid.

17. Seymour Martin Lipset, "Comment," in Laslett and Lipset, eds., *Failure of a Dream?,* p. 528.

18. Stephan Thernstrom, "Socialism and Social Mobility," in Laslett and Lipset, eds., *Failure of a Dream?,* p. 519.

19. Peter R. Shergold, *Working-Class Life* (Pittsburgh, Pa., 1982), pp. 225, 229.

20. James Holt, "Trade Unionism in the British and U.S. Steel Industries, 1880–1914: A Comparative Study," *Labor History,* 1977, p. 35.

21. Michael Harrington, *Socialism* (New York, 1972), p. 116.

22. Quoted in Introduction, Sombart, *Why No Socialism in the United States?,* p. xxiii.

23. Jerome Karabel, "The Failure of American Socialism Reconsidered," in Ralph Miliband and John Saville, eds., *The Socialist Register, 1979* (London, 1979), p. 216.

24. Quoted in Harrington, *Socialism,* p. 131.

25. John H. M. Laslett, "Socialism and American Trade Unionism," in Laslett and Lipset, eds., *Failure of a Dream?,* p. 214.

26. Seymour Martin Lipset, "Why No Socialism in the United States?," in Seweryn Bialer, ed., *Sources of Contemporary Radicalism* (Boulder, 1977), p. 128.

27. Sombart, quoted in Bialer, ed., *Sources of Contemporary Radicalism,* p. 62.

28. Sacvan Bercovitch, "The Rights of Assent: Rhetoric, Ritual and the Ideology of American Consciousness," in Sam B. Girgus, ed., *The American Self: Myth, Ideology and Popular Culture* (Albuquerque, 1981), p. 21.

29. Wendell Phillips quoted in Richard Hofstadter, *The American Political Tradition* (New York, 1948), pp. 139, 159.

30. Antonio Gramsci, *Selections from the Prison Notebooks* (New York, 1971), pp. 21–22.

31. Leon Samson, *Toward a United Front* (New York, 1935), pp. 16–17.

Socialism and Liberalism: Articles of Conciliation?

1. Karl Marx, "The Proceedings of the Sixth Rhenish Parliament," first published in *Rheinische Zeitung,* May 5–19, 1842.

2. Kenneth Minogue, *The Liberal Mind* (London, 1963), p. 150.

3. Friedrich Engels, "On the History of the Communist League," in Marx and Engels, *Selected Works* (Moscow, 1962), 2:344.

4. Karl Marx, "The Eighteenth Brumaire of Louis Bonaparte," in *The Marx-Engels Reader,* ed. Robert C. Tucker (New York, 1972), p. 514.

5. Karl Marx, "Conspectus on Bakunin's *Statism and Anarchy,*" in *Marx-Engels Werke* (Berlin, 1964), 18:599–642.

6. V. I. Lenin, *State and Revolution,* chap. 5, sect. 2 ("Transition from Capitalism to Communism").

7. Minogue, *The Liberal Mind,* pp. 79–90.

Thinking about Socialism

1. Martin Buber, *Paths in Utopia* (Boston, 1949), p. 96.

2. Karl Marx and Friedrich Engels, *The German Ideology* (London, 1942), p. 26.

3. Paul Ricoeur, "Power and the State," in Irving Howe, ed., *Essential Works of Socialism* (New Haven, 1976), p. 736.

4. Stephen F. Cohen, *Bukharin and the Bolshevik Revolution* (New York, 1975), p. 54.

5. Stuart Hampshire, "Epilogue," in Leszek Kolakowski and Stuart Hampshire, eds., *The Socialist Idea* (New York, 1974), p. 249.

6. Karl Kautsky, "The Commonwealth of the Future," in Howe, ed., *Essential Works,* p. 169.

7. Quoted in William English Walling, *Progressivism and After* (New York, 1914), pp. 169–70.

8. Harold Orlans, "Democracy and Social Planning," *Dissent,* spring 1954, p. 194.

9. Leszek Kolakowski, "Introduction," in Kolakowski and Hampshire, eds., *The Socialist Idea,* p. 15.

10. Michael Harrington, "What Socialists Would Do in America—If They Could," in Irving Howe, ed., *Twenty-five Years of Dissent: An American Tradition* (New York, 1979), p. 23.

11. Alec Nove, *The Economics of Feasible Socialism* (London, 1983), p. 174.

12. Radoslav Selucky, *Marxism, Socialism and Freedom* (London, 1979), p. 36.

13. Ibid., pp. 179–80.

14. Abram Bergson, "Market Socialism Revisited," *Journal of Political Economy,* October 1967, p. 656.

15. Nove, *Economics,* p. 200.

16. Ibid., p. 207.

17. Quoted in ibid., p. 204.

18. Selucky, *Marxism,* p. 185.

19. Allen Graubard, "Ideas of Economic Democracy," *Dissent,* fall 1984, p. 421.

20. George Lichtheim, "Collectivism Reconsidered," in Howe, ed., *Essential Works,* p. 757.

21. Branko Horvat, *The Political Economy of Socialism* (Armonk, N.Y., 1983), p. 255.

22. Leszek Kolakowski, "The Concept of the Left," in Howe, ed., *Essential Works,* p. 686.

BOOKS BY IRVING HOWE AVAILABLE IN PAPERBACK EDITIONS FROM HARCOURT BRACE JOVANOVICH, PUBLISHERS

A Margin of Hope

Celebrations and Attacks

Socialism and America

Steady Work: Essays in the Politics of Democratic Radicalism, 1953–1966